S0-BGI-308

DISCARD

William Carleton

Twayne's English Authors Series

TEAS 376

WILLIAM CARLETON
(1794-1869)
Drawing by Michal Ann Cierpik,
from a sketch by C. Grey, A.R.H.A.

William Carleton

By Eileen A. Sullivan

Twayne Publishers • Boston

William Carleton

Eileen A. Sullivan

Copyright © 1983 by G. K. Hall & Company
All Rights Reserved
Published by Twayne Publishers
A Division of G. K. Hall & Company
70 Lincoln Street
Boston, Massachusetts 02111

Book Production by John Amburg

Book Design by Barbara Anderson

Printed on permanent/durable acid-free
paper and bound in the United States of
America.

Library of Congress Cataloging in Publication Data

Sullivan, Eileen A.
William Carleton.

(Twayne's English authors series ; TEAS 376)
Bibliography: p. 130
Includes index.
1. Carleton, William, 1794-1869--Criticism and
interpretation. 2. Ireland in literature. I. Title.
II. Series.
PR4417.S9 1983 823'.7 83-10706
ISBN 0-8057-6862-9

To my colleen dhas dhun Danielle JoAnne
and the colleen bawn Tara Lee

Contents

About the Author

Eileen Agnes Sullivan was born in Brooklyn, New York, on October 4, 1925, attended Catholic elementary schools in Brooklyn and Manhattan, and graduated from Garr Institute High School at Goshen, New York. After receiving a B.A. degree in chemistry at Hunter College in New York City, an M.A. degree in English at the University of California, Los Angeles, and a Ph.D. degree in English at the University of Florida. Dr. Sullivan taught at the University of Florida for nine years. While there, she established the Irish Studies Discussion Circle for the South Atlantic Modern Language Association, arranged a seminar on nineteenth-century Irish novelists for the Modern Language Association, and established the *Carleton Newsletter*.

She conducted a seminar on "Violence in Northern Ireland" at the University of Florida and published the papers in *Conflict in Ireland*. With grants from the University of Florida Graduate School and the American Irish Foundation, she established and published *Eire 19*, a journal of nineteenth-century Irish letters. Dr. Sullivan published a monograph, *Thomas Davis*, for an Irish writers series and articles and reviews for scholarly journals. Most recently, she prepared essays on Carleton, Maria Edgeworth, John Ruskin, W. B. Yeats, Fitz-James O'Brien, Edna O'Brien, Mary Lavin, and Sean O'Faolain for an encyclopedia on short fiction. As a member of the American Committee for Irish Studies, she has lectured on Irish literary subjects at various American universities and continues in that activity.

Preface

To his contemporaries, William Carleton was a genuine bit of old Ireland, a great storyteller, the greatest Irish novelist, and either a hero or a villain because of his partisan position on Catholic emancipation (1829) and the failure of the Repeal of Union Act (1842). A man of many contradictions, he wrote vicious anti-Catholic stories in the religious controversy prior to the passage of the Catholic Emancipation Act after converting from Catholicism to Anglicanism. Carleton also wrote the most powerful novel for the nationalistic cause, *Valentine M'Clutchy* (1845), denouncing the Protestant clergy and the government after publicly apologizing for his impetuous early anti-Catholic short stories.

In 1848 all political parties and religious sects supported Carleton's drive for a British governmental pension. After receiving it, he published *The Tithe Proctor* (1849), attacking Catholicism and the national movement with a greater fury than he had unleashed in the early short stories. His mood swung back to a condemnation of the Protestant clergy and the eighteenth-century government in *Willy Reilly* (1855). This novel also characterized benevolent Protestant clergy and gentlemen who opposed the government. It was not until the latter years of his life that Carleton resolved the religious conflict. He believed that Catholic priests were the most moral of men administering to a moral people. For himself, however, he chose to die as an Anglican, attended by Anglican priests who satisfied his religious needs.

At the end of the nineteenth century during the Irish Renaissance, William Butler Yeats revitalized Carleton's reputation as a realistic writer by saying he surpassed all other writers of the century. Yeats was particularly impressed by Carleton's ironic humor, "clay-cold melancholy," and fatalism which identified him first with Ireland and then with the world. John Eglinton, a critic of the literary revival at the beginning of the twentieth century, appreciated the hard, biting, realistic short stories and novels and the depth of human experience recorded in *The Autobiography* (1896). He told writers to look at Carleton's work for their prose model in order to create works equal to those of the revival poets and dramatists.

Contemporary Irish writer-critics either praised or damned Carleton's work. Benedict Kiely and Patrick Kavanagh belonged to the first category and Frank O'Connor belonged to the second, whereas Sean O'Faolain treated Carleton with benign neglect. The contradictory critical response derived partly from an Ulster versus Munster perspective. Kiely and Kavanagh represented the Ulster viewpoint. O'Faolain and O'Connor, looking at Carleton from a Munster viewpoint, were able to shut out Carleton's vision of Ireland. He wrote of strange sights and northern farmers who spoke imperfectly with voices that arose from the craggy hills. Kiely and Kavanagh, however, accepted Carleton's sights and sounds of pre-famine Ireland as moving pictures of their own culture.

This study analyzes short stories from Carleton's early anti-Catholic period, comparing them to his revised versions, which removed objectionable material. They reveal Carleton's satiric presentation of his people. His later satiric tales did not have to be revised for republication because they met his own artistic demands. Carleton's many novels are of unequal value and document the diversity of his style; an effort has been made to explain the superiority of his greatest novels. A sketchy biography, describing the chaotic conditions of Carleton's life as they related to his art, introduces this study. It concludes with an account of his unfinished autobiography, a moving work of art. His few poems are not discussed because of their limited appeal. Every effort has been made to separate Carleton's indefensible behavior from his work. This was necessary in order to establish the greater importance of the universal nature of his fiction over his sectarian religious sentiments, thus demonstrating that Carleton's tales and novels merit his literary reputation as the father of modern Irish literature.

Eileen A. Sullivan

Acknowledgments

Of the American scholars who have helped me establish Carleton's reputation and disseminate his works, I would particularly like to thank Daniel Casey of the English department at the State University of New York at Oneonta who coedited the *Carleton Newsletter* for several years and contributed critical articles to it. I am indebted to Franklin Doty, former dean of University College at the University of Florida, and Stephen C. O'Connell, former president of the University of Florida, for their encouragement and financial support of my research into the unknown frontier of nineteenth-century Irish studies. Professors Mary Bryson at Montana State College, William Dumbleton at the State University of New York at Albany, Grace Eckley at Drake University, and Maureen Murphy at Hofstra University are early "Carleton fans," and I am grateful for their looking into aspects of Carleton's works that needed definition. To the extraordinary librarians at the University of Florida—Annette Liles, Ray Jones, Virginia Francis, and Sherman Butler—I owe an unpaid debt.

Remembering my trips to Ireland, I am pleased to have this opportunity to thank Ben Kiely in Dublin, Gerald Dawe, the young poet now teaching at University College, Galway, William Bradley at Stranmillis College of Education in Belfast, Terence Brown of Trinity College, Dublin, and Alan Warner at New University of Ulster at Coleraine. Mrs. Mary McKenna, past president of the Carleton Society, and the other members of the society deserve a note of thanks for their willingness to escort me to Carleton's cottage, "Carleton's Leap," and other areas of interest. Through the years, Professor André Boué of the Sorbonne has been a steady source of encouragement and information about obscure points in Carleton's biography and works.

Chronology

Churchyard Bride" (poem) in the *National Magazine*; *Traits and Stories of the Irish Peasantry* (first series, first edition).

1831 Short stories in the *National Magazine* and the *Christian Examiner*; "A Sigh for Knockmany" (poem) in the *National Magazine*.

1832 "The Landlord and Tenant," the *Dublin Penny Journal*.

1833 Short stories in the *Dublin University Review and Quarterly* and the *Dublin University Magazine*; *Traits and Stories of the Irish Peasantry* (second series, first edition).

1835 "Jane Sinclair or the Fawn of Springvale," the *Dublin University Magazine*.

1837 *Skizzen und Erzahlungen aus dem Leben des Irischen Landvolks (Sketches and Stories from the Lives of Irish Country People)*.

1839 "The Three Wishes," the *Dublin University Magazine*; *Fardorougha the Miser or the Convicts of Lisnamona*.

1840 "A Record of the Heart or the Parent's Trial," the *Citizen*; short stories in the *Irish Penny Journal*.

1841 "A Legend of Knockmany," *Chambers' Edinburgh Journal*; short stories in the *Dublin University Magazine*, the *Irish Penny Journal*, and the *Citizen*; *The Fawn of Springvale, The Clarionet, and Other Tales*.

1843 "The Late John Banim" and *"Dublin University Magazine* and Mr. Lever," the *Nation*.

1845 *Art Maguire or the Broken Pledge; Roddy the Rover or the Ribbonman; Parra Sastha or the History of Paddy-Go-Easy and His Wife Nancy; Tales and Sketches Illustrating the Character, Usages, Traditions, Sports, and Pastimes of the Irish Peasantry; Valentine M'Clutchy the Irish Agent or the Chronicles of the Castle Cumber Property;* "Les Chroniques de Château-Cumber au l'agent d'un Landlord Irlandais," *l'Univers* ("The Chronicles of the Castle

Cumber or the agent of an Irish Landlord," the *Universe*).

1847   *The Black Prophet, a Tale of Irish Famine.*

1848   "The Evil Eye," the *Irish Tribune; The Emigrants of Ahadarra;* awarded pension of £200.

1849   *The Tithe Proctor, a Novel: Being a Tale of the Tithe Rebellion in Ireland;* met Thomas Carlyle in Dublin.

1850   Visited London, met William Thackeray and Leigh Hunt; "Black and All Black, a Legend of the Padereen Mare," the *Illustrated London News;* "Willy Reilly and his Dear Colleen Bawn," the *Independent.*

1852   "The Fair of Emyvale" and "The Squanders of Castle Squander," the *Illustrated London News; Red Hall or the Baronet's Daughter; The Squanders of Castle Squander.*

1853   "Master and Scholar," "The Silver Acre," the *Illustrated London Magazine.*

1854   "Taedet me Vitae" ("I Am Tired of Life") (poem), the *Nation;* "The King's Thief," the *Commercial Journal and Family Herald.*

1856   "Fair Gurtha or the Hungry Grass," the *Dublin University Magazine.*

1857   *The Black Baronet or the Chronicles of Ballytrain,* a revision of *Red Hall* (1852).

1860   *The Evil Eye or the Black Spectre;* "The Rapparee," *Duffy's Hibernian Magazine.*

1861   "The Miller of Mohill," the *Illustrated Dublin Journal.*

1862   *Redmond Count O'Hanlon, the Irish Rapparee.*

1868   "The Weird Woman of Tavniemore," the *Shamrock.*

1869   January 30, died, buried in Mount Jerome Cemetery, Dublin.

1896   *Autobiography* published; biography completed by David J. O'Donohue.

Chapter One
From Clogher to Dublin

In the Clogher Valley

James Carleton and his wife Mary Kelly could never have imagined at the birth of their son William, the youngest of their fourteen children, that he would leave the Clogher Valley and acquire a renowned literary reputation in Dublin. The state of Irish affairs in 1794 when he was born to the poor but talented couple in Prillisk, a small farming town in County Tyrone, would hardly favor such a prediction. Politically, all Ireland was an English province on the verge of a rebellion.[1] Four years after William's birth, the failure of the Revolution of 1798 hardened English rule, giving more authority to Orange Lodges, the Protestant repositories of legal and police power.[2] Since Carleton was born to Catholic parents, he automatically would be excluded from voting or running for office. He naturally would be subjected to the jurisdiction of a state in which he was a political nonentity. It was highly unlikely that he would ever assume any role in Irish literature. James and Mary Carleton, consequently, could hardly expect William to become a Protean figure in Irish literary circles.

Carleton's parents were native Irish speakers, versed in Irish folklore, legends, traditions, and music.[3] His father, who could speak English as well as Irish, worked hard and enjoyed a good reputation in the community. It was from him that Carleton learned a great amount of folk material: heroic legends, supernatural tales, and local folklore.[4] The information was transmitted orally in English and Irish. James Carleton was a better English speaker than his wife. She had a fine singing voice but had difficulty in finding English lyrics to suit the Irish music. Their bilingualism was a sign of the continuing erosion of the Irish language in the eighteenth century and the shift from Irish to English for literary expression.

A few years after Carleton's birth, the family moved to

Towney, another small village near Prillisk. William's life as a young child was insecure as his father moved in search of land leases. It was at Towney that Carleton began his education in a hedge school, taught by Patrick Frayne, the model for Mat Kavanaugh in "The Hedge School" (1830). Such schools were impromptu establishments, held along roadsides or in barns donated by farmers anxious to educate their children. With the removal of the Dublin Parliament at that time (1801) to London, stable land leases and proper education were further removed from Carleton's class of people who made extraordinary efforts to educate their children.[5]

There were not enough students to keep Pat Frayne in the area. Within a year Carleton was attending a school operated by Mrs. Dumont, an Irishwoman who had married a Frenchman subsequently killed in the French Revolution. She and her daughter Mary Anne returned to Ireland and opened a school for girls from five to eighteen years of age. Classes were held in a barn, and the Dumonts boarded with the more prosperous farmers. Mrs. Dumont frequently visited James Carleton who entertained her with tales of old Irish legends. She suggested that William, who was about six years old, attend her school. It was a disastrous experience. He fell in love with Mary Anne, who was old enough to be his mother, and wanted to marry her. When the school moved to another barn, William attended until he was expelled for fighting with one of the girls.

For two or three years, Carleton received no formal education because no schoolmaster came to the region. When O'Beirne opened a hedge school at nearby Findramore, Carleton attended it for almost a year. He learned the fine art of making a good shillelagh for party fights between Catholics and Protestants, along with reading, arithmetic, and writing skills. When Pat Frayne returned and opened a school at Skelgy, more conveniently located, William was sent there. A sod house, carved into the bank on the roadside, was constructed for Frayne, and over a hundred Catholic and Protestant students were taught there. This educational system did nothing to change religious prejudices and political realities. Since Carleton was an excellent reader, in his tenth year he directed the Catholic and Protestant students in an inflammatory play dramatizing past battles between their ancestors. He was encouraged by his schoolmaster to do so despite the fact that it exacerbated religious and political bigotry.

In looking back at this period, Carleton recollected the overpowering Protestant police force.[6] The cavalry and yeomen with few exceptions were anti-Catholic men, members of the Orange Society which commemorated the Catholic defeat by William of Orange at the Battle of the Boyne in 1690. It was a common practice for drunken yeomen armed with guns and bayonets to make night visits on Catholic families, forbidden to bear arms, on the pretense of searching for weapons. In the middle of the night, Carleton's family was visited by such a group, an event recorded in *Valentine M'Clutchy* (1845). The incident indicates the nature of the undisciplined police power and the helplessness of the Catholic population.

Not long after the night visit, the family moved to Nurchasy where Carleton attended a hedge school at Tulnavert, operated by Charles McGoldrick who had been expelled from the Catholic seminary at Maynooth because of insanity. The exseminarian was a tyrannical teacher who physically beat and abused Catholic students for minor behavioral problems but ignored the gross misconduct of the Protestant boys. The abusive schoolmaster in "The Poor Scholar" (1830) was modeled after McGoldrick. William attended this school for about three years, even after the family moved to Springtown, a change caused by the agent's failure to transfer James Carleton's rent to the landlord.

Environment certainly played an important role in Carleton's literary life. Autobiographic incidents from Nurchasy and Springtown appear throughout his fiction. Pentland's portrait in "Bob Pentland or The Gauger Outwitted" (1842) was modeled on the middleman at Springtown who handled the rents for the land agent while running an illicit still. While at Springtown, young Carleton acquired the motivation to pursue a writing career, so far beyond the aspiration of his class. He also fell in love with Anne Duffy, the miller's daughter. For over four years, he worshiped her as he knelt opposite her at mass. At her marriage, he experienced all the emotional pain of a rejected lover although he had never spoken to her. To prove himself to her, Carleton was determined to succeed as a writer. It was not until over a quarter of a century later at the height of his fame when he returned to Clogher Valley that she spoke to him of her love for him.

A major change occurred at Springtown with the death of James Carleton. At that time William, about seventeen years old, was neither working nor attending school. He lived with his mother, sister Sarah, and brothers John and James. William suggested, and the family agreed, that he should become a priest. That meant he would be sent to Munster as a poor scholar and be educated for the Catholic priesthood. His family, friends, and neighbors gave him money and supplies for his journey. It was a painful departure, described in "The Poor Scholar" (1833). The journey ended, however, before he reached Munster. At Granard in County Longford, Carleton had a fearful dream in which he imagined a mad bull that was chasing him was about to gore him. Carleton interpreted the dream as a sign that he did not have a vocation. In the morning he walked back toward Springtown[7] and lived with his family as an idle youth for two more years.

The time was not idly spent for an aspiring artist, however, for he read the odd collection of books and pamphlets he found in the parish. Although half of the Catholic population was illiterate, they kept some books for those who were able to read. *The Life of Edward, Lord Herbert* and Defoe's *History of the Devil* were two favorites often found in the cabins. Carleton's search for reading material indicates that his quest for knowledge had not ended. He was a student without a master. Pat Frayne's brief return to the neighborhood afforded little intellectual stimulation because he was teaching arithmetic and science, two fields in which Carleton fared poorly. His artistic aptitude was toward classical studies and literature.

Carleton has not been recognized as an artist who created a new order for himself by destroying the old, but he was creator/destroyer, nevertheless. It was not only Carleton's refusal to accept the spade and the reaping hook as tools for his livelihood that demonstrates his attitude toward the old system, it was also his active search for new forms to express himself that caused his conflict. The more the established social order closed in around Carleton, the more inadequate that order seemed. The aspiring artist looked for other groups to satisfy his need for external order. His individualism evoked a set of circumstances that evolved into a canon that flatly rejected his class system. Since there was no new class into which he could transfer, Carleton experienced all the anguish and alienation common to an artist suspended between two worlds. In pursuit of new forms through which he could align himself to society, Carleton discovered that Father John Keenan, a second cousin, ran a classical school in Glasslough, County Monaghan. After consulting with his family, Carleton set out for Monaghan in 1814 and enrolled at Keenan's school, remaining there for two years while living with relatives and friends. Each month, however, he walked the sixteen miles back to Springtown to visit his family. During one of the walks, he was initiated into the Ribbon Society, a secret Catholic association organized to combat the Orange Lodges. Ribbonism was not the innovative system that Carleton sought. He joined the organization more by default than active pursuit and condemned its activities in "Wildgoose Lodge" (1830).[8] Carleton was more interested in classical studies, and at Glasslough, he was in his element.

He learned to read and write Latin fluently because of Keenan's teaching method of using Latin as the school's language. Carleton could easily translate Latin works and compose English works in Latin. The idyllic existence ended when Keenan left to open a larger school at Dundalk, County Louth. Immediately after this interruption of Carleton's quest for fulfillment, he returned to the Springtown cottage, now occupied by his mother and brother James. Sarah and John had married; the account of his marriage is given in "Shane Fadh's Wedding" (1830). Carleton tried to reconcile the differences between his ambition and his station in life by thinking of opening a classical school at home, but he gave up that idea when he realized only three students would attend. The skills acquired at Glasslough were useless in Clogher Valley, and Carleton faced an uncertain future.

True to his artistic self, Carleton continued to study and to amuse himself at weddings, wakes, and social gatherings. In the process he acquired a reputation as a young priest. He lived up to that preposterous claim, assuming a pedantic place in the community. The women were particularly impressed by his ability to translate Greek and Latin passages while extolling their beauty. Carleton satirized this aspect of his life in "Dennis O'Shaughnessey Going to Maynooth" (1831). While enjoying some social standing, at least with the women, Carleton decided to make a pilgrimage to Lough Derg in County Donegal, a famed penitential site dating from the Middle Ages. The pilgrimage satisfied his need to explore a famous site and to be part of a social gathering. He made it the subject of his first contribution to the *Christian Examiner*, "A Pilgrimage to Patrick's Purgatory" (1828).[9]

His return from Lough Derg in 1817 marked the beginning of the end of his life in Clogher Valley. William would not work the farm at Springtown, and his invalided brother James was physically unable to manage it alone. After losing their furniture and farm, William, James, and their mother moved in with their married sister, Sarah. From then on Carleton had no home. He lived with Sarah, his oldest brother Michael who continually harassed him about his indolence, his father's brother, or illiterate neighbors who wanted to listen to his classical tales. The break finally came when Roger Hacket, Sarah's husband, refused bed and board to the struggling artist after Michael had evicted him. As fate would have it, a few days before Carleton left Clogher, he chanced upon a copy of *Gil Blas* and read it as a true adventure story (*L*, 1:125).

The antiheroic picaro was an acceptable new form to Carleton, filling his needs during an uncertain period. He could accept Gil Blas, whereas he could not accept the model that Michael and Hacket presented. The image of Gil Blas served an important psychological function for Carleton, helping him cope with a severe identity crisis.[10] Thinking about the exploits of Gil Blas, Carleton became a knight-errant on the road to fame. As he walked away from all that he loved and valued, he was alienated from his culture, yet unaccepted by a fresh social order. This dualism dogged Carleton throughout his life in Dublin where he wrote imaginative tales of Clogher Valley without being on firm ground. He vacillated between picaresque good-natured understanding of his people and pontifical vituperative attacks upon them.

Capitulating with bitterness and indignation to a roguish set of ethics, Carleton left Clogher penniless, for Hacket failed to give him so much as a pound note for his journey into the unknown. Without a home behind him or ahead, the Irish picaro walked more than twenty-five miles on the first day to a distant relative's home in Castleblayney, County Monaghan. He was fortunate on his first night because he was well fed, housed in Lord Blayney's shooting lodge, and recipient of a pound in tenpenny bits from the charitable woman before he resumed his journey. Carleton considered the warm reception to be a good omen. He had found an external world where his activities were no one's moral concern. Michael and Roger had both tried to convince William that his quest for artistic achievement was immoral and evil, and he resented their convictions. Getting the pound note in Castleblaney was more significant than getting it from Hacket; it was a stamp of approval for the new life.

Carleton, however, did not rush on to Dublin. He wandered about County Louth for about two years, acquiring the raw material for his fictional tales. In the fall of 1817, he saw the body of Paddy Devaun decomposing in a pitch sack hanging on a gibbet outside his mother's cabin. The vision reappeared in "Wildgoose Lodge."[11] Carleton was beginning to understand more fully Ireland's terrible economic condition. Hitherto, his father and brothers had worked under the corrupt land lease system to provide a cottage for the family. On the open road in Louth, Carleton saw a different response to the corruption. Unlike the peaceful Carletons who accepted the unjust evictions, some men fought back. Men murdered each other, attacking and defending the hopelessly debased system. Carleton viewed more than one Ribbonman's corpse on the gibbets in his wanderings through County Louth.

More fortunate than the executed men, Carleton was hired by Pierce Murphy at Lowtown to tutor his children. Murphy's prosperous farm was the O'Brien farm in *Fardorougha the Miser* (1839), and Mrs. Murphy was Mrs. Burke in *The Emigrants of Ahadarra* (1848). Tutoring children, however, was not what Carleton wanted; he became bored, restless, and frustrated. Following his own star, the tutor frequented the tavern at the crossroads after his teaching assignments and showed some of his poems to the tavern keeper, Peter Byrne, who assured Carleton he had a future in literature. This kind of praise kept his literary ambition alive. At the tavern, Carleton met a

professional piper, blind Gaynor, who played for the gentry
and wealthy farmers. Decades later his counterpart appeared in
"Talbot and Gaynor, the Irish Pipers," *Tales and Sketches* (1845).
Carleton stayed with Murphy for about four months, having
been hired for a year and paid a quarter's salary. When Murphy
refused to pay the extra money, Carleton knocked him to the
ground and went off to Byrne's tavern where he had not the
foggiest notion of his next adventure.

The aspiring artist's decision to leave Lowtown was derived
from feelings evoked after reading *Gil Blas*. They urged him
onward, to take a chance. He hoped that like Gil Blas he might
"come to a calm and safe harbor at last" (*L*, 1:189). Although
reading the tale helped Carleton escape from his banal existence at Lowtown, it entangled him in a new web of reality in
which he freely acted out his fantasy. He was actually trying to
become what he pretended to be, resisting at all costs the
restrictions being placed upon him by the old order. The people
in Lowtown had formed a flattering opinion of Carleton,
believing he descended from a respected old family of a higher
social degree than the Murphys. He worked out their fantasy,
too, in leaving Murphy and Lowtown.

Once that decision was made, Carleton had to move on. The
next stop was an uninvited visit to his cousin, Father John
Keenan, at Dundalk, who told Carleton there was no job for
him in his school and advised him to work. He told Keenan that
he would never degrade himself by working as a day laborer
and with angry words left Dundalk, penniless and hungry.
Walking to Drogheda, Carleton spent a night at an inn where
the landlady took his shirt for payment. To get out of that
difficulty, he boarded a ship on the river and conned some
sailors of money to redeem his shirt by pretending to be a
Ribbonman. Hearing that there was an opening for a schoolmaster in Fane Valley, Carleton temporarily gave up the idea of
going to Dublin and headed back north toward Dundalk.

Not getting the teaching position, he reappealed to Keenan
with the same verdict—go to work. Carleton again refused to
do so and settled into a more artistic lifestyle in County Louth.
He lived with a hospitable innkeeper on the road between
Dundalk and Drogheda and roamed the countryside, telling old
Irish tales and his own stories which he composed during the

day and recited at night around the fireside. The popular storyteller was also well received by families anxious for entertainment, and his reputation grew among the people. They would travel miles to hear him when he was in their neighborhood. This seemed to be the height of his fame, and Carleton was resigned to his situation until he learned of a Catholic boarding school at Navan, County Meath, where he expected to find employment.

During the summer of 1819, he walked to Navan and boarded for three months at an inn where he met Gaynor, an educated tailor who fed, clothed, and encouraged Carleton to apply for a position at the school by writing to the bishop of Meath. Nothing resulted from the inquiry. With Gaynor's departure from Navan, Carleton had to move on. He walked south and decided to visit Clongowes, the Jesuit college in County Kildare. Its literary fame rests upon James Joyce's student days there, not for any assocation with Carleton. Interviewed by a half dozen priests, he was not given employment.

While in the area, Carleton visited Maynooth, the Catholic seminary. He got an unfavorable impression of the curriculum, but he did meet people in the town who were anxious to help him. After his wanderings through Counties Meath and Kildare, Carleton still had not found work. Finally, friends from Maynooth found him a teaching position in Newcastle, County Dublin. He became a hedge schoolmaster to about twenty half-naked children and lived with the grateful farmers. The life of a schoolmaster depressed Carleton, however, and he thought again that something better must be in his future. He did not know what to expect, but the present was causing more pain than pleasure. The schoolmaster was looking back, too, thinking of the better days with his own hedge schoolmaster, Pat Frayne. Without planning ahead, the pattern of his entire life, Carleton left his job at Newcastle and walked on the great southern road toward Dublin. He had two-and-ninepence in his pocket and thoughts of Gil Blas in his head, looking for the safe harbor.

In analyzing Carleton's desultory drive toward literary fame, four observations help explain his later position in Irish letters. First, his early religious feelings were quite normal. They

consisted of acquiring habits of praying and churchgoing, and a
familiarity with Catholic ritual—an ordinary experience for
children with practicing religious parents.[12] Evidence to sub-
stantiate a mature religious sentiment is lacking. At mass, he
was more interested in Anne Duffy than the deity. His vocation
was associated with the pursuit of a classical education, and his
pilgrimage to Lough Derg was performed as a tourist rather
than a penitent pilgrim. Priests and bishops were simply men
who should employ his talents. *Gil Blas* was Carleton's Bible.
Religion was not a problem during his meanderings through
Counties Tyrone, Monaghan, Louth, Meath, and Kildare, and
Newcastle in County Dublin. He lived with and was an integral
part of the rural Catholic population during this stage of his life,
but it was a social affinity, not a religious one.

The second point that has to be made about Carleton's
pre-Dublin years was his continued reliance upon others for
money. He begged and borrowed from family, friends, and
strangers without shame or misgivings. He rather felt that it was
the responsibility of others to support him while he read and
enjoyed the recreational aspects of country life. He was easily
angered when people refused his demand for money, demon-
strated by his abrupt departure from his brother Michael,
brother-in-law Roger, and cousin Father Keenan. Carleton's
devotion to the people who supplied money bordered on
idolatry. He highly praised the men and women who cared for
his physical wants. Good and bad people were determined by
their response to his needs. In other words, Carleton made
moral judgments about people according to their willingness to
advance his ambition.

A third observation is that Carleton was an impatient drifter
without a program of action. He impulsively followed his
emotions which controlled his experiences. He was unable to
devise a method whereby he could move out of the laboring
class without starving or depending upon the generosity of
others. He lived for the day. On more than one occasion, he
gave up work that bored him to pursue another "adventure" in
the manner of Gil Blas. As in the cases when he left Murphy at
Lowtown and the hedge school at Newcastle, Carleton suffered
great deprivations because of his inability to plan. It was not
that he lacked a contingency plan; he lacked a plan to get him

through predictable situations. He left the Clogher Valley with no preparation for the journey, and he did the same thing in moving from one place to another, exercising little care in meeting daily necessities. His awareness of the hospitable nature of country people provided him with some surety that he would not starve along the roadside, but such knowledge does not excuse his irresponsible approach to his own destiny.

The fourth observation and the most important to be gleaned from Carleton's account of his early life is his own belief in his literary talents which was strong enough to separate him from his family. He resisted the efforts of his brother and brother-in-law to make him part of the laboring class in Clogher. Just as firmly, he ignored the advice of Father Keenan to take up the spade and work the earth along with other classical students who performed menial tasks. Whenever he was discouraged, recognition of his artistry was enough to change his mood. The people whom Carleton met at the tavern during his tutorship of the Murphy children, who believed he was of a higher social order than his employer, reinforced his belief. Although Carleton had to play many parts, a sign of the way in which his artistic self was duped by society, fundamentally he preserved the writer's role for himself. This amazing fact demonstrates that he wanted to express himself in art outside the moral restrictions of his society. He desired that role above and beyond other social roles: son, brother, tutor, storyteller, knight-errant, and hedge schoolmaster. By assuming the writer's character, Carleton paid a heavy price, for he was poorly prepared for the part he would play in Dublin's literary circles.

There was no opening for him into the literary world with its own class consciousness. The aspiring artist had neither influential friends in Dublin nor letters of introduction to the people who could help him. He had to search for options that would allow him to continue his reading and to experiment with his writing. In changing his religion, Carleton took the most obvious option to a man with such shallow religious convictions. Looking around him, he saw that the Anglican church was firmly established; it was not until 1869 that it was disestablished, the year of Carleton's death and the demise of the *Christian Examiner*. This church offered opportunities to Carleton that would bring him closer to his goal but further away

from his youthful religious practices. With nothing to lose and
everything to gain, he became an Anglican, although in later
years he also sought the company of Catholic priests and
enjoyed their friendship. In *The Autobiography* (1896), he
generously judged the Irish Catholic clergy to be a moral class
of men, an opinion supported by his intimate association with
them. It should be clear that the conversion was not a negation
of his former life; it was a tool to be used in lieu of the spade
that he despised.

The religious change did not change his demands upon
others for money, which became an obsession when his poor
business sense brought him to financial ruin on numerous
occasions. Carleton was unable to give up the idea that because
he had talent others must support him. When his literary fame
was at its height and his pocketbook at its emptiest, he railed at
the nation, expecting it to support him and his numerous
children and grandchildren. This incessant, unreasonable demand, which Carleton assumed to be quite reasonable because
of Irish tradition, alienated him from his Dublin friends,
publishers, and tradespeople. The behavioral pattern had been
fixed in his mind early in life when his Clogher friends and
family and the country people supported him long beyond the
normal limits of dependency. This lifestyle was brought along
to Dublin and executed with success, although Carleton was
never satisifed because his expectations were always greater
than his means.

His lack of self-reliance, then, was a trait acquired from youth
which colored his existence in Dublin. Carleton's financial
dependency led him to make impulsive choices which damaged
his literary reputation, causing men like Thomas Davis and Sir
Charles Gavan Duffy to rescue Carleton from himself. Fortu-
nately, his talent was enough to survive the many unpleasant
experiences that would have destroyed the gift in another man.
Despite the fact that the Clogher countryman yearned to be a
great artist, on attaining that ambition his impulsive dependent
nature robbed him of any satisfaction. In his old age he valued
his athletic feats in Clogher more than his literary works in
Dublin. Leaving the Clogher Valley, although essential to his
literary life, was a much more distressful experience than
Carleton originally thought. He looked back upon his youth as

a golden age. Arriving in Dublin and living there for almost half a century were painful experiences for which Carleton never found the anodyne.

Dublin Years

Dublin was more like the Firth of Forth at rip tide than a safe harbor in which Carleton could drop anchor when he arrived there in 1820. The city was politically unstable, economically unsound, and morally corrupt. He found an urban slum inhabited by degenerate human characters. Street beggars, wandering minstrels, and charlatans replaced his rural acquaintances of working men and women and hospitable innkeepers. Although both groups were equally poor and disenfranchised, the rural people possessed a sense of place and dignity absent in the urban paupers. Carleton's discovery of this world of lost souls, practicing all sorts of deceit to maintain a standard of living below that of a stabled Dublin horse, filled him with horror and disgust. It was with them that he had to pass his first nights because he had no money for food or lodging elsewhere.

He marveled at the ingenious perversion of their intellects as they posed as cripples so they could beg in the streets where shoppers and tourists supplied their meager income. Even more startling to Carleton was the language with which the beggars communicated with each other. It was neither English nor Irish since Carleton knew both tongues, and it was hardly Latin or Greek, also understood by him and unlikely to be spoken by slum dwellers. No doubt, this Dublin dialect was a combination of English, Irish, and original words used as a secret code, but the language was of no interest to Carleton. He was not going to be trapped with such people and left their company as quickly as possible.

The new Dubliner wandered about searching for a teaching post and made another surprising discovery. There were few respectable schools in the city, and many of them were of poor quality. "Nearly one half were hedge schools," Carleton wrote, "taught in private rooms by men, who are unworthy to be compared for a moment with the great body of the country hedge schoolmasters of Ireland" (*L*, 1:199). Thus, he reached two conclusions in comparing Dublin with rural Ireland: the urban poor were of a lower quality than their country counterparts and the schoolmasters were inferior to the rural teachers. This new life was going to be a series of surprises and setbacks to Carleton as he measured past rural experiences with his present urban experiences.

New dimensions were added to his comprehension of Irish life. He had expected to find Dublin a cultural center and a place of opportunity, but it was a city without a sound educational system or economic prosperity. After enduring so many struggles to reach Dublin, Carleton learned that the real struggle had just begun. He also realized the improbability of his achieving instant recognition of his talents. Consequently, he had to adjust to the strangeness of the city and his own obscure place in it. The loss of identity, separation from family and friends, failure to find a teaching position, poverty, and isolation were factors that would have broken a weaker man. Gil Blas and Anne Duffy were not enough to sustain him.

There was another consideration that prevented his returning home or to his familiar haunts in Counties Louth, Meath, or Kildare. He wanted to fulfill the prophecy of an old Scotch gypsy fortune-teller who had said, "He will never be a priest; he will love the girls too well; but when he grows up, he will go to Dublin, and become a great man" (L, 1:213). Because of this, he suffered losses in Dublin, but remained there to work out his destiny after exhausting possibilities of success within his own cultural environment. One crisis followed another. Carleton slept where he could find cheap lodgings and moved frequently for nonpayment of rent, living off handouts from charitable Dubliners. He still refused to work at menial jobs or as an unskilled laborer because of his literary ambition. The fact that the ambition survived under the harsh reality of Dublin underscores the great faith he had in his own talents. As the inexperienced son of a northern Catholic farmer trying to jump class and religious barriers in a city determined to uphold the Protestant ascendancy, Carleton had little chance of becoming a great writer.

Carleton's first real break came when he was hired by Mr. Fox, a Protestant evangelist who operated one of Erasmus Smith's schools, to tutor his son. He was also housed and fed without cost by the Foxes for over two years. While he lived there, he fell in love with Jane Anderson, who was Fox's niece and ten years younger than himself. They were married in 1822 after Carleton was given a clerkship at the Sunday School Society. The couple continued to live gratuitously at the Foxes for six months.

Carleton argued with Fox and was evicted from his home with pregnant Jane locked in their former room. Jane then left her uncle's home to live with her mother, and the expectant father got a room in an eating house across the street. On November 3, 1822, their first child Mary Anne was born, but the family could not be united until Carleton found another job. Carleton lived with William Sisson who worked at Marsh's library. He learned that Carleton was sick of Dublin and wanted to teach at one of the country Protestant schools. He sent him to Dr. Wilson, Director of the Association for Discountenancing Vice, who supplied the Protestant clergymen with schoolmasters.

Both Sisson and Wilson had seen specimens of Carleton's essays and believed the young writer had a literary future. He was sent to the Protestant parish school in Mullingar, County Westmeath, in the heart of Ireland to teach "sixteen or eighteen of the most wretched-looking creatures" he had ever seen (*L*, 1:265). This situation displeased him, and if it were not for Jane's practicality, he would have left that day. As it was, they all remained there for about two years until Carleton was jailed for debt. After that episode, the family returned to Dublin, and Carleton was reassigned to another school at Carlow in County Carlow south of Dublin. He was unhappy there because of the unhealthy living conditions and again returned to Dublin.

At this stage Carleton's autobiography ends. Very little is known about him until his short stories, which he wrote under a pseudonym, appear in the *Christian Examiner* (1828). It is known, however, that Carleton joined the Protestant cause and shamefully wrote against his former coreligionists prior to the Catholic Emancipation Act in 1829. The good people were the Protestants who supplied money; the bad people were the Catholics who were upsetting the good people. Consequently, with his pen, he passionately defended their political convictions. Carleton's letter to William Sisson on November 3, 1826, is the most damaging document about his role in the political struggle.[13] In it, he tied Catholic emancipation to the interests of its most violent supporters and blamed Ireland's ills upon the leadership of the Catholic Association (founded in 1823) and the priests. The fiery language used to describe the clergy—black, malignant, designing, treacherous, false, revengeful, hateful—was symptomatic of his need to keep the Protestants in power. He told Sisson that as a father, he would rather see his children buried than under the yoke of Rome. There is no doubt that Carleton meant what he wrote. The Protestant evangelicals had helped him, and he was doing his best to help them. Any loyalty that remained from his earlier association with Catholicism was lost in asserting his allegiance to Protestantism.

Carleton wrote to Sisson at a time when Dublin was a political cauldron, stirred by Daniel O'Connell and the Catholic Association which was the focal point of the movement. Prior to O'Connell's confrontation with the crown, concessions to the Catholic population were made by Protestant Irishmen led by Henry Grattan, the first Protestant leader with liberal convictions. "No Irish Protestant before Grattan recognized that the freedom of Ireland must mean equal freedom for all the Irish."[14] Grattan, however, argued at the end of the eighteenth century in Dublin before the Irish Parliament was moved to Westminster by the Union Act of 1801. O'Connell argued at Westminster demanding Catholic civil rights, but he organized the Catholic nation from Dublin. By holding great public meetings, O'Connell "used the cause of emancipation to inspire the Roman Catholic masses,"[15] but he threatened and unsettled Carleton who was indebted to the Protestant evangelicals.

While Dan O'Connell was mobilizing the Catholics, Carleton was discrediting him, the clergy, and the Catholic poor. Yet he knew from past personal experiences of the hardships of the rural population and the urban slum dwellers. They were bound by restrictive laws and governed by the Protestant ascendancy determined to extirpate Catholicism. In the battle against Catholic emancipation, Carleton was a villain. André Boué said, "Il est certain que Carleton y joua un role sans dignite" (It is certain that Carleton played here an undignified role).[16] That ignoble role, however, kept Carleton in favor with the Anglican church which employed him; the alienation from the Catholic church was necessary to maintain that position. He had no intention of losing his position and used his knowledge of the Catholic culture to vilify it.

Carleton's association with the Protestant cause continued, and his literary debut was the two-part publication of "A Pilgrimage to Patrick's Purgatory" in the *Christian Examiner.* This journal whose full title was the *Christian Examiner and Church of Ireland Magazine* was founded in 1825 by Reverends Caesar Otway and Singer to propagate Anglicanism and to expose the evils of popery. For Carleton, the journal served as his means to the literary life for which he left the Clogher Valley and Catholicism. Caesar Otway was his mentor, literary agent, and source of income as more anti-Catholic stories appeared in the journal. Otway's influence upon the writer was considerable. For an imaginative writer of Carleton's background, Dublin without Otway offered little opportunity for Carleton to develop his undisciplined talents. Had he lived in the eighteenth century, he would have had to cross the Irish Sea and trust to his luck in London as other Irishmen and Scotsmen —Goldsmith, Swift, Boswell, and Smollett—had done. In the nineteenth century, though, with the establishment of the *Christian Examiner,* supported by the established church which was supported in turn by the government in Dublin Castle, writers for the cause found a ready reading public. Carleton, by writing for an ecclesiastical Dublin journal, was establishing a reputation as an Irish writer. This was important to him. Naturally, Carleton's career was affected by the intent of the stories written under Otway's guidance because of the perspective from which the stories were written. However, without Otway to instruct Carleton in the art of journal writing, he may not have developed his talent and become a man of letters.

The oral technique of storytelling was more conducive to Carleton's style. He had heard stories from his father, listened to others' tales around firesides during his knight-errantry, and effortlessly composed his own stories for villagers' entertainment. Writing his stories, meeting deadlines, and obeying editors' precepts was something new for the countryman whose education and training had been so haphazard. Although the four-year apprenticeship with Otway created a rift with the

Catholic population, the learning period was essential for Carleton's literary development.

But to remain any longer with Otway would not benefit Carleton who was acquiring a reputation quite different from the one he imagined. Otway's restrictions on Carleton's style were felt as unnecessary obstacles to his literary development, which meant that he had to find other publishers who were more concerned about literature than religion. The *Dublin University Magazine* with its fresh approach to Irish society after the passage of Catholic emancipation offered Carleton the opportunity to write for a broader, less biased audience. He contributed some of his finest fiction to that journal, the natural vehicle for artists who were consciously creating literary works. It was the proper outlet for Carleton whose work in the *Christian Examiner* had been compromised for the past four years. He was now free to practice his craft according to the dictates of his artistic conscience, and he moved away from religious propagandizing.

Following his release from the *Christian Examiner*, Carleton serialized several early novels in the *Dublin University Magazine*. During the 1830s, Carleton, for a change, was making more friends than enemies by his steady inoffensive contribution to the new journal. Sir Samuel Ferguson, a noted lawyer and poet who contributed to the publication, was one of the new friends and one who remained loyal to Carleton throughout his long career. Their walking tour in County Wicklow which took them through the glens and over the Wicklow mountains that inspired Synge was one of the pleasurable experiences of the early years in Dublin. Ferguson commemorated the event in a short poem, "Pretty Girl of Loch Dan," which highlighted their stop at a cottage where a young girl refreshed the weary travelers with a bowl of sweet milk and buttered oat cakes.

In 1836, Ferguson and Carleton went on another walking tour to North Wales, an enjoyable experience. They were close to nature and rambled at will throughout the countryside. Mrs. Jane Carleton was at home, of course, caring for their many children while her husband enjoyed the gentleman's pursuit of pleasure. These excursions with Ferguson indicated the lifestyle that Carleton wished for himself: it was carefree and close to nature. He walked the fields rather than worked them; that relationship with nature was ideal for the man from Tyrone. The walks were not material for Carleton's art as they were for Ferguson; they were respites from Dublin's environment. Carleton's imagination was stimulated by memories of his Clogher Valley and Knockmany Mountain; he included very little from outside that magic kingdom in his fiction.

During the 1830s, Carleton made the acquaintance of Michael and John Banim and corresponded with them, exchanging views about their literary roles and opinions about "King Dan," Daniel O'Connell, who was organizing and working for political reform, which was beyond Carleton's comprehension.

While most of Carleton's tales and novels of the 1830s appeared in the *Dublin University Magazine,* some brief character sketches of the dancing master, the fiddler, the midwife, the matchmaker, and other rural types appeared in a short-lived journal, the *Irish Penny Journal* (1840–41). Petrie and Dr. O'Donovan, Irish antiquarians, also contributed to the periodical. Carleton enjoyed the friendship of George Petrie and Dr. John O'Donovan who added to Carleton's knowledge of Ireland although he was not particularly fond of the class of antiquarians. These men were available to Carleton when the new annotated edition of *The Traits and Stories* was issued in 1842. Dr. O'Donovan briefed Carleton about the history of the Reillys when Carleton later decided to develop a novel around the ballad of "Willy Reilly and His Colleen Bawn."

After his success with the short story and the novel, Carleton, a frequent theatergoer from his early days in Dublin, wanted to write a play. He was induced by J. W. Calcraft (the pseudonym of John William Cole), who was actor-manager of the Theater Royal in Dublin, to write for the stage. Carleton's "The Irish Manufacturer or Bob Gawley's Project" opened on March 25, 1841, but closed in a few nights; only the prologue is extant. It dramatized the living conditions of the Dublin poor, their suffering, and their working conditions, but playgoers reacted unfavorably to it. Had Carleton dramatized his own successful *Fardorougha the Miser* (1839), the result may have been different. It had previously played for a longer period at one of the smaller Dublin theaters, being dramatized by Anne Jane Magrath without his consent. Presenting the Dublin poor to Dublin dwellers was not the key to dramatic success, as Sean O'Casey learned, even though the lives of the slum dwellers were filled with dramatic moments. Carleton had earlier expressed a desire to dramatize Thomas Dick Lauder's *Rival Lairds of Strathspey* and was given permission by the Scotch novelist in 1837 to prepare the novel for the stage, but nothing came of the desire. "The Irish Manufacturer" was Carleton's sole dramatic work, and it has little literary value.

With the establishment of the *Nation* in 1842, Carleton acquired another publishing outlet as a substitute for the *Dublin University Magazine,* which was edited in 1842 by Charles Lever whom Carleton accused of plagiarism. The conservative periodical published nothing by Carleton until the end of Lever's editorship; the *Nation,* however, with its nationalist policy became an important source of income for Carleton after Sir Robert Peel refused Carleton's request to pick up John Banim's pension after his death in August 1842. Carleton on September 23, 1843, published "The Late John Banim" in the *Nation* in which he praised his fiction, contrasting it with the inferior work of Lever who trampled upon truth and debased Irish life by his disgusting caricatures of Irishmen and women. Banim's work, according to Carleton's article, was also greater than that of Anna Marie Hall, whose Irish characters spoke a monstrous language with an emasculated vocabulary, punctuated by stolen bits of Irish phrases from authors who knew the Irish language. On October 7, 1843, Carleton again attacked Lever in the *Nation,* criticizing his editorship of the *Dublin University Magazine* which according to Carleton was so dull no one read it. He also charged Lever with habitual plagiarism, ridiculed his characterizations, and blamed him for the English failure to appreciate Irish society because of his outrageous defamation of the Irish character and lifestyle. These comments from Carleton, who had previously attacked the Catholic clergy as well as the country people for their customs, traditions, and social mores, were actually addressed personally to Lever who, in Carleton's mind, denied him publication access to the magazine. Lever's fiction, written with a comic approach, hardly deserved such a vituperative attack, but since the author offended Carleton, he turned his pen against Lever's character, his fiction, and his editorship.

The nationalist fire burned in Carleton's mind as he wrote *Valentine M'Clutchy* (1845) under the influence of Thomas Osborn Davis and Charles Gavan Duffy. In the same year, Carleton also published three other novels: *Rody the Rover or The Ribbonman*, *Art Maguire or The Broken Pledge*, and *Parra Sastha or The History of Paddy-Go-Easy and His Wife Nancy*. His last work of 1845, *The Tales and Sketches of the Irish Peasantry*, was printed by James Duffy who published more of Carleton's work than any other printer. This book included the stories previously published in the *Irish Penny Journal*, fantastic stories of folk origin, and many realistic stories. If Carleton had been properly compensated, this tremendous output should have alleviated his financial distress, but James Duffy paid Carleton only twenty-eight guineas for *The Tales and Sketches* and ten guineas if it went to a second edition. He was equally underpaid for the other works. He earned at the maximum about £150 per year for his work during his lifetime, an incredible fact considering the quantity of his literary creations and the many editions of his popular works. Marie Edgeworth and Tom Moore, for instance, earned more than £1000 for one of their popular works. In writing to support Carleton's pension, Edgeworth advised him of the necessity of retaining his copyright, but the advice came too late. In any case, it would have been difficult for Carleton to follow because he was always in such financial distress that he had to accept the publisher's pennies to meet his daily living expenses.

Nearly at the top of his literary career in 1846, Carleton selected that time to return to famine-struck Clogher Valley, about thirty years after his hasty departure. His seventy-year-old brother Michael was a gaunt, worn, emaciated man whose appearance startled Carleton. He was pleased, however, with his visit to Anne Duffy, his cousin John Carleton, and his reception in the community. Prior to his return to Clogher, Carleton had finished *The Black Prophet* which was published in the *Dublin University Magazine* in 1846, and it seemed the right time to renew his home contacts because he thought this novel was his greatest work.

Returning to the conservative press did not sever his ties with the Young Irelanders. When Thomas Carlyle visited Ireland in 1847, he met with the Young Irelanders in Dublin. Carleton was invited to a breakfast held in Carlyle's honor. A spirited argument arose about Shelley's poetry which Carlyle denounced but Denis Florence McCarthy praised; Carleton agreed with Carlyle. This surprised the group because it was unaware of Carleton's knowledge of English poetry and nonfictional prose. Carleton developed a warm relationship with Michael Doheny and Thomas Francis Meagher, Young Irelanders who were later exiled from Ireland and served brilliantly in the American Civil War.

In 1848 Carleton wrote "The Evil Eye" for John Mitchel's *Irish Tribune*. Mitchel, the leader of the violent wing of the national movement, was exiled and jailed in Tasmania for treason. He wrote a valuable history of England's oppression of Ireland as well as the most literary account of the national cause in his jail journals. But when Carleton's pension was being reconsidered, he disassociated himself from Mitchel's editorial policy. When the £200/year pension was granted by the Whig government in 1848, Carleton paid his past creditors over the next three years while going into debt with new creditors. The heavy debts depressed him. He was chided by Lady Wilde, Oscar's mother, who was an ardent nationalist and a contributing poet to the *Nation*. She found Carleton brooding about his finances when the aborted Revolution of 1848 had destroyed the national movement and exiled or executed the Young Irelanders with whom he had been closely associated.

Lifted out of his depression, Carleton went to London in 1850 and managed to get other novels published but at little profit to himself. While there, however, he was well received in literary circles, meeting people who thought he looked and wrote like Sir Walter Scott. Carleton revived his friendship with Samuel Lover who had been a frequent visitor at Carleton's Dublin home. He also met William Thackeray and Leigh Hunt and dined with them. Since Dickens was not in London at that time, Carleton did not make his acquaintance. He later wrote on two occasions to Dickens about contributing to his *Household Words*. Dickens responded in 1854, asking Carleton to send samples of his work, but nothing appeared; nor did the two meet in Dublin when Dickens visited Ireland.

Most of the 1850s was spent fitfully in Dublin where Carleton's despondency overwhelmed him after the emigration of his three daughters to Canada. In his grief he wrote a poem "Taedet me Vitae" (I Am Tired of Life) for the *Nation,* December 30, 1854, recollecting Ireland's neglect of him, John Banim, and Gerald Griffin and speculating about joining his family in Canada to find happier days. More readers complained about Carleton's imagined distress and Ireland's shameful treatment of him than were impressed by his expression of loneliness, for Carleton with a guaranteed pension of £200 per year was far ahead of thousands of Irishmen who could not earn £50 per year. In his declining years, Carleton continually attacked anyone and any institution that did not respond to his needs. He tarnished the reputation he had acquired by his many works and felt that he had no country because it did not regularly praise and honor him.

Giving up the idea of emigrating to Canada, Carleton was attracted to Belfast where in 1859 he held a disastrous public reading of his works at the invitation of Dr. T. C. S. Corry. Carleton in 1863 wrote to Corry, requesting a gift of £30 to pay his life insurance premium for the £1000 policy purchased over fourteen years before. Returning to Belfast in 1864, Carleton was trying to get "Anne Cosgrave," a novel, published. Although the attempt was unsuccessful, he made friends and thought of moving there. Meanwhile, on his return to Dublin, he tried again to get an appointment for his son John, who had failed his Civil Service examination for a clerkship at the post office. At the same time, the author was looking for an increase in his pension to £250 or £300, but the British prime minister, Benjamin Disraeli, refused because of more pressing demands upon the public treasury. Writing to John McKibbin in Belfast in 1865, Carleton said his policy was almost lost again, but he wrote to Dublin's Sir Benjamin Guinness who remitted the necessary money.

Toward the end of his life, Carleton thought his reputation was greater in the north than in the south, west, or Dublin where he was not attuned to the rising commercialism. Yet a following in the capital city honored his accomplishments. At a public meeting in Dublin in 1866, Carleton learned he was to share the stage with a juggling act and would have stormed out had it not been for his daughter Jane. It was an impulsive wish similar to his desire to leave Mullingar which had been thwarted by his wife Jane. Staying at the Winter Palace, Carleton learned he was appreciated in Dublin because the committee moved him to a raised gallery. When his name was announced, a scene ensued that had had no equal since the days of O'Connell. Thousands of people shouted, stamped their feet, and crowded around him as he left the hall, acknowledging his fame. It was a satisfying experience for the aged author whose need for public acclaim was always very great and whose sensitive heart was so easily crushed.

Just as Carleton's impulsive, sensitive nature remained unchanged during the Dublin years, so did his naive approach to publishers. Unfortunately, no literary agent or friend ever came forward to intercede for him in handling the printing and distribution of his work, and his last association with a publisher was disheartening. In 1867 Richard Pigott, the unscrupulous editor of a Dublin periodical, the *Shamrock,* asked Carleton to compose stories for seven and sixpence per page and to allow the republication of stories from *Traits and Stories.* After "Neal Malone" and "Phil Purcel" appeared in the *Shamrock* in January and February 1868, Carleton learned he did not own the copyright. It was held by William Tegg, an English publisher, who had bought the copyright from another publisher and had printed editions of *Traits and Stories* in 1864 and 1865. Pigott had to reimburse Tegg for infringement of the copyright. Carleton, astounded by the fact that he did not own the two stories from the first series in 1830, agreed to give Pigott manuscripts that he had on hand to cover his loss. Two very different stories, "The Weird Woman of Tavniemore or The Milking of the Tethers, a Tale of Witchcraft" (April 1868) and "The Romance of Instinct" (February 1869) were published in the *Shamrock.* Neither of them equaled the tales written during the early Dublin years when his vision of the world conjured the thatched cottage, the earthen floor, and the poorly furnished homes of people who ate food cooked over turf fires and sat around the hearth in the evening listening to the legends, tales, and romances of an ancient culture.

With an unusual amount of emotional control, Carleton wrote *The Autobiography* out of a sense of commitment to himself, knowing that his death was imminent. He completed only the most important part: his parentage, family life, education, wanderings, marriage, and conversion to Protestantism.

Calmly facing death after deciding he would not return to Catholicism, Carleton on his deathbed was attended by Reverend Mr. William Pakenham Walsh and Reverend Mr. Leet of the Sanford Anglican Church in Dublin, which he had frequented during the last eighteen months of his life. At the same time, he had often met with Jesuits at Miltown Park, Father Richard Carbery being a favorite. Carleton was actively seeking a religious faith toward the end of his life. Although Father Carbery believed that Carleton would revert to the faith of his fathers, the author consciously chose to die as a Protestant. It was not an impulsive decision reached on the spur of the moment; to the contrary, it was made out of a regard for his salvation and the religious sentiments of his wife and daughters. Carleton advised Father Carbery of his decision, thanked him for his spiritual advice, and hoped they would meet again in the presence of the "Father of us all." Carleton's peaceful death ended a lifetime of strife, spent in the elusive search for the ideal state.

Chapter Two
Stories in the *Christian Examiner*

An Apostate's Remembrance

Carleton's first contribution to the religious journal recalled his Lough Derg pilgrimage and was entitled, "A Pilgrimage to Patrick's Purgatory" (1828). Although it defames Catholic Ireland, its revised version, "The Lough Derg Pilgrim," which appears in *Traits and Stories* (1843), remains a favorite. This and the other tales that Carleton wrote for Otway would not have established a literary reputation because Otway was not a critic who could judge the stories according to prevailing literary criteria. He suggested Lough Derg as a topic, for he believed Carleton could handle the subject because of his familiarity with Catholicism. The story of the pilgrimage was published from Otway's perspective with long passages of religious significance important to him and the readers of his journal but of no value to a literary public. In the introduction to the 1843 edition of *Traits and Stories,* Carleton admits that the 1828 version which he wrote in four days had been altered by Otway, who told him, "I will dress it up and have it inserted in the next edition."[1] Carleton also states that the revised edition is similar to the earlier publication "with the exception of some offensive passages which are expunged" (W, 2:797).

The extent of Otway's "dressing up" and the authorship of the expunged passages have been controversial subjects among Carleton's critics. Professor André Boué of the Sorbonne believes that Otway wrote part of the story: "Les plus notables sont l'introduction et une portion assiz longue du dernier paragraphe" (The more notable are the introduction and a long portion of the last paragraph).[2] Benedict Kiely, thinking it impossible "to determine how many of the offensive passages came originally from Carleton's pen, how many were added by

Otway's editing,"[3] is convinced that Otway wrote part of the story. Daniel Casey agrees with Boué and isolates other passages which he attributes to Otway.[4] Margaret Chesnutt disagrees with Boué, Kiely, and Casey and imagines Carleton wrote the entire story. She does, however, notice that the intention stated in the introduction, which was to expose superstitious practices of Catholic pilgrims, is not always carried out. "But in spite of this intention the story maintains for the most part a humorous tone, only slipping into polemic shrillness now and again."[5] Thomas Flanagan hears two voices—one of a pedantic preacher and the other of a romantic pilgrim—but he does not investigate further.[6]

Most probably, Reverend Caesar Otway wrote the polemic anti-Catholic passages ridiculing Catholic dogma while Carleton composed the anecdotes of the pilgrimage since he lacked intellectual religious beliefs and the evangelical fervor to introduce his tale in this fashion: "It is melancholy to perceive the fatal success to which the Church of Rome has attained, in making void the atonement of Christ by her traditions; and how every part of her complicated, but perfect, system, even to the minutest points, seizes upon some corresponding weakness of the human heart, thereby to bind it to her agreeable and strong delusions."[7] While Carleton could, as evidenced by the Sisson letter (1826), write anti-Catholic sentiments to his Protestant friends, they express his support of Protestantism rather than analyze Catholic doctrine. Otway was more apt to write, "It is strange, indeed, to what lengths a Roman Catholic priest may go . . . before his conduct is considered improper. . . . Drunkedness is nothing—swearing is nothing"(*CE*, 6:353). Carleton exposed priests' vices and shortcomings, but he did not condemn them as a class.

"A Pilgrimage to Patrick's Purgatory" is a disjointed tale told by two discordant voices for the conservative evangelical readers of the *Christian Examiner*. For literary unity, however, one voice must prevail. Carleton decided it would be his own in the revision and deleted almost fourteen hundred words from the introduction. He also omitted the slanderous reference to his dead father who is pictured as a greedy man anxious for the overthrow of Protestantism. "He enumerated what the income of a bishop might amount to, under the present dynasty; but should emancipation pass, and things turn out as was expected, why the Palace of the Protestant bishop of ____, would be, he would add smiling placidly, no uncomfortable residence for me" (*CE*, 6:271). Actually, most Irish fathers considered a vocation to be an honor rather than an economic matter to the family, and this characterization of an avaricious father lacks verisimilitude. Carleton exercised his literary judgment and deleted this passage in "The Lough Derg Pilgrim." He also cut out passages that describe the authority of the Catholic church to be treacherous, deceitful, and tyrannical, including a long section beginning with "Oh, Romanism! Romanism! the blood of millions is upon you—you have your popes, your priests, your friars, your nuns, your monks, . . . but you have not Christ " (*CE*, 6:350). About twenty-five hundred words were deleted from "A Pilgrimage to Patrick's Purgatory" to make the twenty-nine-page "The Lough Derg Pilgrim" a unified tale.

Carleton's unusual literary partnership with Otway ended with the publication of "Dennis O'Shaughnessy Going to Maynooth" (1831) when the conflict became so strong that the bonds between them ruptured. But in that interval, Carleton published a total of thirteen tales for the *Christian Examiner*. Understandably, the revised first and last contributions to the journal with their heavy emphasis on autobiographic material, "The Lough Derg Pilgrim" and "Dennis O'Shaughnessy," acquired lasting fame. More than a century and a half has passed, but these mock-heroic exploits continue to amuse and entertain. They have outlived the purpose for which they were written and have achieved a sense of universal belonging.

"A Pilgrimage to Patrick's Purgatory"

The narrator of "A Pilgrimage to Patrick's Purgatory" (1828) is a blurred carbon copy of Carleton who was skillfully recollecting incidents from his own pilgrimage. Fine characterizations and descriptive imagery, coupled with a mastery of the Irish idiom, develop the plot which revolves around the activities of a central figure. In this case, it is the narrator who is a nineteen-year-old on a pilgrimage. With the sermonettes removed, the tale moves along rapidly as the naive young man experiences one adventure after another during the journey. As a lover of natural beauty, he is at ease with God and man, and his vision of the countryside determines his mood. "The sun looked down upon all nature with great good humour . . . across the upland country, which stretched down from a chain of dark rugged mountains. . . . the scene was exhilarating" (*CE*, 6:273).

The unnamed narrator overtakes two women on the road who mistake him for a priest, and he describes their attire: "dressed in grey cloaks, striped red and blue gowns; drugges, or linsey-wolsey petticoats, that came within about three inches of their ancles" (*CE*, 6:276). They travel together toward Lough Derg. The spirited dialogue between the pilgrim and the women record their relationship. He speaks perfect English, whereas they express themselves in an Irish-English dialect with numerous usages of Irish phrases and greetings. After they stop at a pilgrim's inn (many of them were open only during the summer months when pilgrimages were made), the young man notices his companions have not eaten breakfast and asks them if they are going to eat. "No, avourneen machree (darling of my heart)," the older woman says. Before he knows what he has done, the young pilgrim pays for their breakfast before they journey on. Along the way, he sees small groups of more pilgrims and hears their chatter, observing an air of abstraction about them despite their differences in character and costume. Conversations cease and a general hush comes over the crowd as it reaches Petigo, a town about four miles from the lake. The narrator also feels the religious awe, terror, and enthusiasm. In spite of these emotions, he is disturbed by his admiration of the natural wonders of Lake Erne and his inability to distinguish between the mountains and clouds in the distance. He comes back to reality and joins the crowd pushing toward the town.

At a lodging in Petigo, the young pilgrim closely examines the others and observes a range of guilt and religiosity among them. Men with pale faces and drooping eyelids or plump rosy faces and black twinkling eyes are described, as well as severe and self-sufficient faces. He sees humorous, lascivious, avaricious, pompous, and ignorant senile men, but also observes genuinely pious people who pray alone.

In church the pilgrims see a dim light coming from two candles upon the altar and hear the steady, monotonous, supernatural hum from the voices of about six hundred sleepy, praying pilgrims. The young pilgrim enters the macabre meeting room to begin his prayers. When he nods, he is awakened by a blow to the head dealt by an old man. In forcing himself to keep awake, his mind wanders and he loses his sense of reality, believing he has become insane. He groans and shrieks along with others, and the unholy din unnerves him. About two o'clock in the morning, one young man from fear and fright throws himself from the gallery and dies from his injuries. After this break in the night's routine, people are sleepy again, and when gentle nudges and pulled ears fail, they must be hit by other penitents walking about for that purpose. The young narrator becomes an awakener and with great gusto whacks the head of the old man who had hit him. Prayers are led by a man with a harelip whose native tongue is Irish. Between the nasal tone and the misuse of English, praying takes on a comic character with the priests and prisoners laughing at the leader.

The light of the sun finally restores a naturalness to the interior, and the people, whose souls are heightened to a new spirituality, go on to another event. It consists of rewalking upon the stone spikes while praying. The people may drink the unclean lukewarm lake water, but they cannot eat. Then they return to the church until midnight when another group replaces them. Once allowed to sleep, the weary pilgrims fall into a stupor and awaken with refreshed spirits. They confess their sins, receive the Eucharist, and offer prayers for one another. While swapping prayers, the narrator meets Sol Donnel, a perennial pilgrim who tells him, "You've the sogarth [priest] in yer very face" and offers the "grey profungus" (de profundis, out of the depths) in exchange for tenpence (CE, 6:355).

The next episode, also present in the revised version, detracts from the main story. It chronicles a priest's contemptuous treatment of an elderly man and his son who are sick and weakened by their journey. The priest takes money from the pair needed for their return home, and the young pilgrim tries to get it back. The priest reaches for a cutting whip to beat him but decides against it and asks his assistant to eject the youth who had been ready to depart after his encounter with the salty

Sol Donnel. It is mid-afternoon, and in the boat he joins his female companions. They decide to walk farther than Petigo for better lodgings known to the older woman. Once there, she inquires about the hour of his morning departure. Sleeping late, he finds his hat, coat, and waistcoat missing, replaced by the old lady's ragged jacket and hareskin cap. It does not take him too long to discover that the attentive old crone also stole most of his money. For the remainder of the trip, he walks along, looking more like a poacher than a priest.

At home, the family greets him with a request for a blessing. The members fall upon their knees for there is a special grace connected with a Lough Derg pilgrim's blessing. He distributes to them pebbles from the lake, and the family feels elated by the blessing and the sacred bits of stone. It is not until he attends Sunday mass that he learns the thief's identity. His priest laughingly says, "So, you have fallen foul of Nel M'Callum the most notorious shuler [tramp] in the province—a gipsey, a fortune-teller, and a tinker's wife" (*CE*, 6:362). The perplexed parishioner learns that he is not the first she has deceived, but he must beware of her the next time. The young pilgrim assures the priest there is no danger of a second encounter, and the story ends with his having gained some knowledge of the world.

"A Pilgrimage to Patrick's Purgatory" identifies Carleton as a remarkable regional writer whose future fame rested upon his characterizations of individuals known from his youth. Carleton's comic presentation of his adventurous people gives a sympathetic view of what could have been a condemnatory story. In mildly satirizing the gullible pilgrims, Carleton pokes fun at himself. He is not removed from his people; on the contrary, the narrator is a part of that mass of humanity that has experienced major losses, the most grievous being the loss of the Irish language with its ancient literary accomplishments. The pilgrim praying in a language he does not understand symbolizes social upheaval and the distressed condition of the country people trying to adapt to change. The social significance of "A Pilgrimage to Patrick's Purgatory," or "The Lough Derg Pilgrim" as it is called today, outweighs its former polemic importance. The young pilgrim, Sol Donnel, and Nel M'Callum

have become respectable literary characters while the wicked
priests and the machinations of their church have faded into
oblivion.

"The Broken Oath" and "Father Butler"

Unlike the former tale, "The Broken Oath" (1828) has no
redeeming social grace to rescue it from its anti-Catholic bias,
and it has not been reprinted outside the *Christian Examiner*.
Henry Lacy is the central figure, but he does not relate his
story; it is told instead by an old schoolmate. Lacy's father is a
wealthy respectable farmer who ignores his son's moral education. Although Lacy exhibits a moral sense as a boy, it is gone
when he matures because of his association with vulgar laborers
and dependence upon the Catholic sacramental system which
forgives his sins without correcting him. At twenty, Lacy is
managing a farm that produces the best barley in the region,
which he illegally converts into alcohol at a stillhouse in a
remote section of the farm. He attends mass, teaches the
catechism when not intoxicated, and believes in the infallible
authority of his church. His devotions increase with the increase in his criminal behavior. To counteract the Protestant
political power, Lacy joins the Whiteboy Society, a Catholic
terrorist association similar to the Ribbon Society. When his
father dies, Lacy inherits his entire estate, marries, and intends
to reform. Despite his frequent confessions, though, he cannot
change his criminal behavior. When his income suffers because
of his continued drunkenness, Lacy calls in his neighbors and
"on his knees pronounced an oath . . . binding him for fourteen years . . . not to taste spirits or any other liquid capable of
intoxicating him" (*CE*, 6:433). He observes the oath for five
years, and his affairs improve until his meeting with Father
Bernard.

The priest invites Lacy into a tavern and tells him he cannot
absolve him of his oath for the coming nine years, but he can for
the day. They drink, but Lacy continues to drink for another
five days and is brought home in a violent rage. In a passionate
fit, Lacy throws a stool at a servant who is bringing in his son to
pacify him. The servant ducks; the child is struck and dies in his
father's arms on the next day. Lacy never recovers his former

temperate state, going back to illegal distillation and Whiteboy-ism. His farm is raided by the police searching for whiskey, and the disturbance leads to the death of Mrs. Lacy and their infant son. Lacy and his three daughters are evicted and must live in a hovel. The half-crazed brooding man with help from his brother-in-law then kills the gauger who raided his farm. Lacy is caught, jailed, and sentenced to death.

Providentially, a Protestant chaplain visits the condemned criminal and converts him, giving him spiritual comfort and peace of mind. Shortly thereafter, Father Bernard arrives "with a most ill-timed smirk upon his face. . . . 'Harry, my dear fellow,' said he, 'how do you do? I'm glad to see you'" (*CE*, 7:35). Lacy repulses him because the priest has made him a perjurer and a sinner with the constant confessions and absolu-tions. With courage derived from the minister, Lacy faces his hanging with confidence in God. He refuses to confess to the Catholic chaplain or receive the last rites and dies a Christian death. On the platform, Lacy tells the chaplain, "I look on death as the entrance to happy eternity—but my orphans—teach them the truth and protect them" (*CE*, 7:39). In three years, the three daughters are buried beside their father. The broken oath has destroyed the entire family.

Neither characterizations nor dialogue are up to Carleton's standard in this tale. Lacy's life and death occur without his developing individualism, and the story reads like a case study. The most tender and memorable scenes take place in the jail among Lacy and his daughters, Jane, Mary, and Anne (the names of Carleton's daughters). Other scenes are flat colorless pictures drawn to illustrate the evils of Catholicism. The unbelievable conversation between Lacy and Father Bernard in the jail does not serve a literary purpose, but illustrates Otway's notion of Catholic priests. There are dramatic incidents in the tale, but the action is secondary to the examination of Lacy's dependence upon a sacramental system that evokes such behav-ior. The emphasis upon the Protestant ethic as opposed to Catholic corruption detracts from the literary potential of Lacy's downfall. Carleton reworks this plot in "Larry M'Far-land's Wake" (1830) to create a moving story. The same plot appears in *Art Maguire or The Broken Pledge* (1845) and *The History of Paddy-Go-Easy* (1845) written from a Catholic per-

spective while Carleton is under the influence of the Young
Ireland nationalistic movement.

"Father Butler" (1828) is told in a long rambling fashion by a
Protestant landowner in Carleton's Clogher Valley. The
seventy-eight-page narrative appears in five issues of the *Chris-
tian Examiner* and attacks several Catholic characters before
Butler's tragic history unfolds against a background of tainted
Catholicism. Deviating from geography, Carleton moves
Clogher to County Kildare, the site of the Jesuit College at
Clongowes, and introduces a scheming Jesuit into Butler's life.
Butler is a noble Catholic youth engaged to Ellen, the virtuous
daughter of his Protestant neighbor, Mr. Upton. Both parents
agree to the marriage until James falls ill and then recovers by
miraculous means. The Jesuit convinces the Butlers that their
son had been spared so that he can enter the priesthood, but
young Butler disagrees with the conclusion until the Jesuit
dupes him into believing that Ellen is interested in a former
suitor. At his mother's deathbed, James vows to keep the oath
she made to God during his illness that he would enter the
priesthood.

James vacations at home and discovers Ellen has not changed
her feelings; on the contrary, she is hopelessly in love with him.
Since he is bound to his oath, he resists her. Ellen dies eight
days after his ordination, and her mother follows her four days
later. Father Butler is so distressed that he cannot accept a
parish and lives with his father, visiting Ellen's grave day and
night where the narrator meets him. In time, Father Butler
recognizes the folly of his oath and the wickedness of the
Catholic church, especially after the Jesuit cajoles the elder
Butler to leave his farm to the Jesuits. James convinces his
father to change the will, frees himself from the priest's
influence, and joins the Protestant church shortly before his
death. Old Mr. Butler moves to Dr. Upton's home, and the two
fathers bemoan the loss of their families because of the evil
nature of Catholicism.

The importance of "Father Butler" lies within the many
interruptions in Butler's story which introduce country characters caught in the religious confrontation between Catholics
and Protestants. Paddy Dimmick, an ignorant defender of the
Catholic faith who argues with the landowner, is such a

character. Throughout the story, Paddy praises Catholic ritual and practices, and when the landowner asks him if place makes a difference in the power of prayer, Paddy says, "To be sure it does, Sir, or what 'ud bring us to Lough Dearg?" (*CE*, 7:119). References within the tale to the Protestant effort to convert the Catholic country people (the proselytizers were known as Biblemen in rural Ireland) document the fact that Dublin was not the only battlefield. Ironically, this unhappy romance is the source of much information about Catholic practices and rituals in rural nineteenth-century Ireland. It also records the extent of the very serious attempt to Protestantize Ireland which included the printing of Bibles written in Irish. "Father Butler" has had a short reprinting history and does not form an integral part of Carleton's meaningful fiction.

"The Station" and "The Death of a Devotee"

"The Station" (1829), under the supratitle of "Sketches of the Irish Peasantry, Nos. 1–3," emphasizes Carleton's artistry rather than his apostasy. The tale, appearing in three issues, has more dialogue and sharper characterizations of his countrymen, hence, the supratitle. Father Philemy M'Guirk and his parishioners are the memorable characters in this tale, which dramatizes a common religious occurrence among the country people —a station, which "simply means the coming of the parish priest and his curate to some house in the townland" (*CE*, 8:47). The tale begins with M'Guirk's announcement during Sunday mass of his intended visits for the week. Thursday's station at Phaddhy Sheemus Phaddy's is the subject of the narration, and his cabin is the focal point of the activities.

Social customs along with religious practices are explained, for instance, Phaddhy's name. His surname is Doran, but because many people have that name, he is called after his father and grandfather for identification purposes. Phaddhy is the son of Sheemus who is the son of Phaddhy. The son of Phaddhy is Brian Phaddhy Sheemus Phaddhy. To Phaddhy and his wife Kate, a visit from Father M'Guirk and his curate Father Con M'Coul is an unexpected honor although an expected expense. The couple is anxious to have Father M'Guirk quiz Brian—who is destined for the priesthood because of his

understanding of Latin. Great preparations precede the station
so that Brian and the other ten children may profit from the
experience. Phaddhy and his six sons are fitted for new suits by
Jemmy Lynch, "the bandy tailor, with his two journeymen, and
three apprentices, sent for in all haste" (CE, 8:54). Carleton
describes their hurried work in outfitting so many in such a
short period of time while frenzied cooking, cleaning, and
rearranging is going on in the cabin.

The anticipated day comes, and Father Con enters to
"Musha, Kead milliah farltha ghud!" (Indeed a hundred thousand welcomes to you!) (CE, 8:119). Before long he is hearing
confessions of neighbors and wandering beggars who hear that
a station is going on at Phaddhy's house. The kitchen is the site
of Father Con saying mass and giving the Eucharist to the
confessed people. At the festive dinner, Father M'Guirk fends
off Protestant Dr. Wilson's inquiry about the Bible: "Me, an
enemy to the Bible! No such thing, Sir . . . we are met here as
friends . . . and must relax a little; we can't always carry long
faces like Methodist parsons" (CE, 8:435). At the end Phaddhy,
discovering M'Guirk's ruse which shamed him into buying wine
and mutton for the dinner, says he is glad he did it because
everyone had such a pleasurable evening.

"The Station," because of its depiction of country life, is one
of Carleton's better-known stories. After deletions of about
eleven pages of anti-Catholic sentiment, it became part of *Traits
and Stories* (1830), the first edition of the first series, and
innumerable subsequent editions. Father M'Guirk's actions,
although they seem disreputable, are consistent with the behavior of country priests. He is a social and a religious character.
Consequently, the anti-Catholic bias does not overpower the
story, which is essentially a description of the station from its
inception until after the gala dinner when clergy, family, and
neighbors assemble.

The spirit of the congregation conveys the gaiety and humor
of Carleton's Catholic people. The fine characterizations of
Father Philemy, Phaddhy, Kate, Brian, and their neighbors
reveal the paradox that was Carleton's own: the subjection of
those he loved to Otway's defamation of them. In this humorous satire of a religious custom, the praise and damnation are

easily separated, and the edited version of "The Station" becomes one of Carleton's great stories.

In "The Death of a Devotee" (1829), the anti-Catholic bias dominates the tale which is written to slander the sacrament of extreme unction given to dying Catholics, as "Father Butler" attacked holy orders and "The Station" abused penance and communion. The plot consists of Father Moyle's visit to dying John Lynch who wishes to receive the last rites in order to be absolved from punishment due to his sins. The character of Father Moyle who is seventy-six years old is not clearly delineated, nor is his association with Lynch and the narrator who is living in the priest's home. It appears that the old priest harbors serious doubts about the Catholic church and inwardly accepts the Protestant view of salvation. But he is weak, influenced "by the force of erroneous opinions long wrought into his duties and habits" (*CE*, 9:268) and fears the exposure of a past transgression involving Lynch who was his servant for fourteen years in France. Therefore, the venerable old man remains within the Church sorrowfully working out his relationship with God.

The night of Father Moyle's sick call to Lynch is a wild one: a rare hurricane storms through the parish. The tempest matches Moyle's reaction to the demand that he, and only he, attend Lynch's deathbed. The priest raises his arms convulsively and his distorted face becomes deathlike. His brows are lifted wildly in fright, and "the pupils of his eyes are almost turned inward, as if the fearful vision which he contemplated was grappling with his own spirit" (*CE*, 9:272). The inner storm subsides. Father Moyle composes himself and sets out in the turbulent night for Lynch's mud house. There, the dying man who had been a devotee, or voteen—a parishioner who fasted, prayed, and sacrificed—awaits the priest's arrival. He fails to convince Lynch to die as a Protestant trusting in God's mercy and will not administer the last rites because "there is none but the God Christ Jesus, who redeemed you by his most precious blood, who can give you absolution" (*CE*, 9:279). The family tries to force the old priest to give the sacrament, but he falls into a stupor. The conflict is resolved by the appearance of Moyle's curate who administers extreme unction; Lynch dies

happily, but not before making his brother promise to under-
take three Lough Derg pilgrimages.

Although the polemic nature of "The Death of a Devotee"
detracts from its literary value, the realistic account of the
tempestuous night and the deathbed scene attests to Carleton's
skill in describing natural settings and salient features of the
poor country people's lives. Stripped of its doctrinal trappings,
this sixteen-page story can be a dramatic presentation of an
Irish priest's response to a dying man's spiritual needs because
it does picture the priest's responsibility to the people and their
expectations of him. However, confused Father Moyle who
refuses his duty and the caricature of John Lynch whose body is
laden with scapulars and the cords of St. Francis with pagan
charms around his neck and a crucifix in his hands convey a
distorted reality. Because of the unexplained relationship between the perplexed prelate and the ludicrously drawn devotee
plus the distortion of reality, the tale lacks artistic merit. Its
only reprinting by William Curry, the publisher for the *Christian Examiner,* in *Tales of Ireland* (1834) divulges the limited
impact of "The Death of a Devotee."

"The Priest's Funeral" and "The Brothers"

"The Priest's Funeral" (1830) describes the death and funeral
of Father Moyle which occurs about five weeks after Lynch's
death. Because of the old priest's leaning toward Protestantism,
he is under house arrest by the bishop's orders. However,
Moyle's letter to a Protestant clergyman secretly sent by a
trusted servant reveals the conversion. This information is
withheld from the public, and a huge funeral for the popular
priest ensues. Several unpleasant episodes between the Protestant minister and the Catholic clergy, which reveal a benevolent
Protestantism, occur outside the dying priest's room. The
bishop and his underlings are pictured as avaricious men who,
although differing about the distribution of Father Moyle's
material goods, make the Church's claim upon his possessions.
In addition to avarice, the Catholic hierarchy is pictured as
deceitful for it plans a solemn requiem mass for the priest who
died in the Protestant faith. During the procession to the
churchyard, the wild and pathetic Irish keen (death wail) is

heard from ten thousand voices for miles over the countryside, "rising and falling in a melancholy cadence according to the modulations of the dirge" (*CE*, 10:140).

This tale reappears in *Tales of Ireland* (1834), but disappears after that reprinting. The excessive condemnation of the Catholic clergy weakens the story as does the unending praise of the rational Protestant minister who calmly outmaneuvers the bishop in doctrinal matters. The redeeming quality arises from Carleton's description of the funeral attended by Catholics and Protestants who are honoring the memory of a charitable, peaceful man. The tale also demonstrates the author's technique of identifying man's fate with natural phenomena. This time Carleton links the priest's death with a magnificent aurora borealis on the same day. The fine descriptive passages, however, are not enough to raise the literary reputation of the story which has been rarely read beyond the narrow limits of its original audience.

Under the supratitle of "Sketches of the Irish Peasantry," Nos. 4–7, Carleton, in "The Brothers" (1830), attacks another sacrament of the Catholic church—matrimony. He narrates the unhappy events in the wretched lives of Protestant Peggy Graham, Catholic Dan Gallagher, and their sons Tom and Ned. Peggy, a good Protestant woman, is attracted to Dan because of his money. Without her parents' consent, she runs away with him to Harry Moran's cabin where a make-believe priest marries them. The Catholic sentiments about mixed marriages are divulged by the members of the wedding party sitting about Harry's fireside. It is believed that a Catholic woman who marries a Protestant, "if she doesn't get him to turn, lives with one on earth, who will be the devil's partner hereafter" (*CE*, 10:207), and most of their husbands convert. The Catholic clergy, consequently, favors mixed marriages for the conversion rate is just as high with Catholic husbands who exercise greater control over their Protestant wives. Peggy's minister is aware of the pressure that she will experience to change her religion, knowing well "the arts and expedients resorted to, for the purpose of bringing heretics in such circumstances into the pale of that Church without whose limits, her followers believe, there is no salvation" (*CE*, 10:288).

The rest of the story, like Maria Edgeworth's moral tales,

develops contrasting characters in the subplot to reinforce the examples set by Peggy and Dan Gallagher. The couple has five children, three girls who die in childhood and two sons, opposite in character, who reach manhood. Tom, like his mother, is pious and educated by Mr. Levin at the Protestant school; Ned, resembling his father, is wild and semieducated by Nulty the Catholic hedge schoolmaster who indoctrinates him into the secret Ribbon Society. Peggy is alarmed by Ned's criminal behavior and pleads with Dan to correct him, but he links the correction with her conversion, saying, "I'll tell you what—if you'll come to mass I'll reform him; that is, if you'll turn over to us, body and bones" (*CE*, 10:367). She does not convert, to the disgust of Father Dorneen who advises Gallagher to send her back to the Grahams. The divided family suffers a cruel fate. Dan becomes a drunkard and beats Peggy. Ned is executed for his crimes, and his mother dies shortly after the burial. Dan dies three months later in the arms of Tom who has become a Protestant minister.

In "The Brothers," Carleton showed he could tell a story. The description of the runaway marriage—a recurrent theme found in "Alley Sheridan or The Irish Runaway Marriage" (1830) and many of the novels—is accurate, although it is used here to illustrate the evil nature of mixed marriages. Reverend Otway was unable to preach a sermon better than this to warn Protestant Irishmen and women about the tragic consequences of intermarriage with Catholics. In serving Otway's purpose, Carleton only partly served his own. The black-and-white portraits of Catholics and Protestants are drab, uninteresting characterizations of very colorful people.

The tale appeared in four issues of the *Christian Examiner* and has had a short publication record with just one reprinting in *Tales of Ireland* (1834). The moral of the story is too closely associated with a virtuous exclusive Protestantism. The tale lacks dynamic characters to warrant a literary value. However, it does demonstrate Carleton's ability to develop a story around an idea and then draw characters to embody that notion. In its particular time, the idea must have satisfied conservative evangelical New Reformers, and its characters were formed for missionary propaganda. In *Valentine M'Clutchy* (1845), Carleton performed the same function for Catholic nationalists but achieved a greater measure of literary success.

"Lachlin Murray and the Blessed Candle," "The Lianhan Shee," and "The Illicit Distiller"

Although many Catholic countrymen, including Carleton himself, were unhappy with their existence and the continuing conflicts in Ireland, the plot of "Lachlin Murray and the Blessed Candle" (1830) under the supratitle of "Popular Romish Legends—No. 1" ignores those facts. It works out Otway's thesis that the poor Catholics "lived in peace and ignorance, therefore, and were happy" (*CE*, 10:598). Lachlin Murray from County Tyrone is the central character whose superstitious nature is the source of his ignorance and bliss. With the death of his father who was a weaver, Lachlin becomes so involved with religious rites that he loses the looms and almost starves to death while praying for a miracle to fill his empty meal barrel. His uncle in County Monaghan who has a weaving shop hires Lachlin who regularly visits his mother by walking the eight miles between Tyrone and Monaghan. This means he must cross the mountains that run longitudinally between the counties—a feat that Carleton often accomplished during his student days. On one particular night, Lachlin has some strange experiences while walking over the mountains and through the glens. Although he fears ghosts, he undertakes the journey late at night because one superstition cancels another. "His dread of ghosts . . . was overcome by his confidence in the holy candle given him by his mother, and in a certain prayer against evil spirits, that had been taught him by his father" (*CE*, 10:603). Well armed, Lachlin confronts his adversaries. He wrestles with a horned devil with cloven feet, and sees apparitions of a lake monster, the Virgin Mary, his mother, and St. Patrick before waking up and realizing he was dreaming.

The short tale documents Carleton's continued use of his boyhood memories to ridicule the beliefs of his own family in order to meet his obligations to Otway. The device of a dream within a tale to explain fantastic adventures was used more effectively in "The Three Tasks or The Little House Under the Hill" (1830). Carleton here used his knowledge of Irish folklore to compose a folktale which is inoffensive to any religious creed. In "Lachlin Murray and the Blessed Candle," on the other hand, the folk beliefs are associated with the evils of Catholic rituals and the ignorance of the rural Catholic population. The tale justifies the heroic attempts of the New Reformers to eradicate Catholicism and replace it with a rational Protestantism, but its bias lessens its literary value.

"The Linahan Shee—an Irish Superstition" (1830) exposes and denounces a mixture of pagan and Catholic rituals practiced to safeguard the physical and spiritual health of the people, especially from "being overlooked by evil eyes" (*CE*, 10:846). A confrontation between Mary Sullivan and a haggard-faced woman with a lump on her shoulders covered with a red cloak sets in motion a series of episodes that reveal the superstition about the *lianhan shee* (literally, a "fairy follower" but similar to a succubus). When the parish priest is asked by Mary's husband, Bartley Sullivan, and his neighbors to rid the parish of the weary woman identified as a lianhan shee, he refuses to discuss the issue. The people then get Father Philip O'Dallaghy, who supports himself by miraculously curing their diseases, to meet with the woman in Sullivan's cottage. He demands that she identify herself. To the amazement of all present, she reveals herself to be Father Philip's wife whom he abandoned, and the lump on her back is the nun's robe worn before her seduction. On learning her identify, Father Philip takes her to his home. On the next morning, he is found near the fireplace "burned to a cinder, except his feet and legs, which remained as monuments of, perhaps, the most dreadful suicide that ever was committed by man" (*CE*, 10:861). The woman goes mad and dies some years later.

"The Lianhan Shee" has had an interesting history, reappearing with some deletions and additions in the second series of the *Traits and Stories* (1833) and in subsequent editions throughout the nineteenth and twentieth centuries. The introductory eight lines of poetry describing an evening's calm were omitted; in addition, spelling and grammatical changes were made in the 1833 edition. In the *Christian Examiner*, the weary woman says to Mrs. Sullivan, "you're doin' what's not right in axin' me a question" (*CE*, 10:849), in *Traits and Stories*, she says, "You're doing what's not right in asking me a question"

(*W*, 2:965). Several short paragraphs that prepare the reader for the denouncement are introduced in the revised edition; they describe the woman's anguish and her need for understanding: "She appeared an object of deep compassion" (*W*, 2:968).

Skeptical reactions to "The Lianhan Shee" evoked Carleton's defense of his tale in both the *Christian Examiner* and *Traits and Stories*. A footnote in the journal states "that the manner of Father Philip's death is true—and that his name, residence, and the other circumstances . . . have been known to me from my boyhood" (*CE*, 10:939). In the *Traits and Stories*, he is more expansive and explains in a long footnote that a priest guilty of a great crime may save himself by self-sacrifice. Among the people, legends are told about such priests, and he relates the legend of "The Young Priest and Brian Braar" for illustration. He also remarks that the belief about the lianhan shee was dying out, but his tale is appropriately entitled since among the people any priest's paramour is known as a lianhan shee an sogarth (a fairy follower of the priest). With the additions and deletions, the revised tale acquires credibility and literary merit. Both the suffering priest and his wife become tragic human characters rather than examples of lascivious priests and nuns. The unified plot unfolds more smoothly once the motivation for the wandering woman's behavior and the priest's immolation are given, and "The Lianhan Shee" attains a high rank among Carleton's tales.

The predictable plot of "The Illicit Distiller or The Force of Conscience" (1830) tells the story of Alick Hagan, a murdering Catholic countryman plagued with a guilty conscience. In eleven pages, Carleton describes the location of a still hidden in the mountains and Hagan's murder of Mr. Stinton, the gauger searching for the still. When his body is discovered, it is "in a state which, were it not for his clothes, would have made recognition difficult, if not impossible" (*CE*, 10:934). A reward for the capture of his murderer is announced, but no one betrays Hagan. He marries about a month later but cannot escape the guilt associated with the crime, and his life is a series of sorrowful events. His wife, mother, and children die at separate intervals. Confessing to the priest brings no comfort, and Hagan exists in fear of being discovered. Twenty-two years later on a sleepless night, he returns to the scene of the crime and sees Stinton's ghost. It drives him mad and to his death, and having "lived without God, he died without hope" (*CE*, 10:939). The tale has a moral purpose. The author lets the readers in on the secrets of violent Catholics who, although they may circumvent the law, cannot escape their consciences. "Lachlin Murray" and "The Illicit Distiller" reappeared in *Tales of Ireland* (1834) and then passed into oblivion. More apt descriptions of Irish Catholic pagan beliefs without the Protestant bias are scattered throughout the *Traits and Stories* (1830, 1833) and the novels written in the forties. The illicit distilling is handled more artistically and convincingly in "Bob Pentland or The Gauger Outwitted" (1840) and "Condy Cullen or The Excisman Defeated" (1845).

"The History of a Chimney Sweep" and "The Materialist"

"The History of a Chimney Sweep" (1831) narrates the tale of John Nowlan from his apprenticeship as a chimney sweep to his scheduled execution for robbery. He is the son of an unnamed genteel Protestant man and a vulgar, selfish, hard-drinking domestic, Miss Nowlan. Her husband dies more from shame than from sickness, leaving her four children. His family take all but the youngest away from her; she threatens to knife anyone who removes John, for he has agreed to stay with his mother. Mother and child become destitute, and on cold nights, she sleeps upon damp straw "with her arms about her lonely boy . . . as he lay shivering, famished, and crying for food" (*CE*, 11:279).

She goes to Dublin fifteen miles away to a filthy cellar with her seven-year-old son, and begs during the day and drinks at night. Street urchins taunt John who refuses to associate with them, and the mild, quiet, loving boy is beaten by his mother because he does not fight back. In a dramatic scene, she lashes out at Frank Branagan, the master sweep, about his children calling John a beggar's brat, but in the next instance she is sitting in Branagan's cellar drinking with him. She leaves after selling John to Branagan for a guinea and the use of two Branagan children for begging. Several memorable scenes follow: John's pleading with his mother, the chivalric death of a young boy cleaning a chimney in John's stead, and Branagan's brutal method of instructing chimney sweeps. John's bruised, battered, and ulcerated body survives the incredible cruelties of his childhood, but he becomes a victim of the chimney sweep's cancer. It is a painful condition, so advanced that within three days, "his bowels will drop out of him" (*CE*, 11:290). After being convicted of highway robbery, he dies in prison from the disease before his execution. However, he is comforted in jail by the Protestant chaplain whom John discovers is his brother.

This story has never been republished, although it is a moving account of Dublin's poor. It is unique in that it describes urban impostors, beggars, drunkards, body snatchers (Branagan sells the bodies of his dead apprentices and of John's mother), and uneducated criminals. There is no direct attack upon the Catholic church, its sacramental system, or its clergy; the blame for such ignominy is placed upon the rich, insensitive, and proud Dubliners who ignore the cries of the wretched poor. The story is not a usual part of Carleton's canon since it does not narrate the history of country people. The harsh realities of Dublin's slum dwellers did not become the exclusive subject of Irish fiction until immortalized by O'Casey and Joyce, but Carleton preserved a small segment of their earlier existence. Like most of his rural tales, "History of a Chimney Sweep" depicts one episode based upon an actual event. In this instance, it is the death of the chimney sweep who is caught in the chimney and suffocated by fallen soot; the tale was founded upon Patrick Walker's death on October 7, 1824, while sweeping a Dublin chimney (*CE*, 11:287).

The confused plot of "The Materialist" (1831) combines bits and scraps of folklore with Carleton's use of country characters to tell the story of Alick Henderson, the materialist, or disbeliever in immortal life, and a follower of Voltaire. Maria Edgeworth's *Castle Rackrent* affords some of the background. Alick is the grandson of a frugal Scotch steward to an extravagant Irish gentleman whose estate is bought by Alick's father, known as the "Miser of Fardrum." Young Alick, however, is a spendthrift and a seducer of women, markedly different from his moral twin brother James who inherits the estate. Alick's wickedness includes the murder of his infant son born to an unmarried mother, and the murder of James, made to appear as an accident. Eventually, Alick feels some remorse and travels to Europe to raise his spirits. He does not succeed and retires to a Catholic monastery upon his conversion to Catholicism. He dies having never regained peace of mind despite fastings, whippings, and penitential austerities. His uninhabited Irish home, according to the "active fancy of our superstitious pesantry" (*CE*, 11:532), is the locale of Alick's ghost, conspicuous for its white hair. Like Father Philip in "The Lianhan Shee," Alick sees his hair turn white overnight. In his case it followed the murder of his twin brother. Alick interprets it as a mark of Cain rather than a redemptive sign.

This short story appears only in the *Christian Examiner.* Aside from its importance as a religious propaganda tract, the tale has little significance. The minor characters, the Irish nurse and Scotch housekeeper, offer some comic relief, but they are not part of the action and present a contrived attempt to add substance to the story. Characteristically, Carleton appeals to the anti-Catholic prejudice of his readers, and in this story, he also plays to their bias against the Scottish Presbyterians. There are more weaknesses than strengths in the narrative—a disconcerting plot, poor characterizations, and a fuzzy conceptualization of materialism in Alick's life—which account for the poor reception of the tale beyond the readership of the *Christian Examiner.*

"Dennis O'Shaughnessy Going to Maynooth"

Carleton's last contribution to the *Christian Examiner,* "Dennis O'Shaughnessy Going to Maynooth" (1831), discloses some of the conflict between author and editor that surfaced when Carleton disagreed with Otway's judgment. According to Otway's introduction in the first installment, the sketch "illustrates the smart aptitude for controversy—the overwhelming self-sufficiency—the bloated phariasaical superciliousness which mark the Romish sacerdotal characters in Ireland. . . . The picture is a caricature" (*CE*, 11:686). In the second installment, according to Carleton, Dennis's character is realistic. "His figure, without a syllable of exaggeration, (or caricature—good Mr. Editor) was precisely such as I am about to describe" (*CE*, 11:766). In another interruption which never happened in the twelve tales previously published in Otway's journal, Carleton states his intentions: "I am not writing, Mr. Editor, for a class, nor a purpose; I am not writing to please you nor any man; but I am drawing life as I knew it; as it passed before my eyes—if I succeed in this I am satisfied; if I fail I am satisfied still. I hold not the leading pen of your magazine, and am, consequently, contented with a more humble share of approbation" (*CE*, 11:776).

Carleton is arguing for artistic freedom, Otway, for dogmatic conformity. The editor wins the argument and, in a concluding statement, publicly advises the author of other options. "We are sorry that want of space has obliged us to contract this narrative, and do violence to the manuscript and perhaps the author's desires; but the necessity is imposed on us to close with the concluding number of the year, an article which has occupied so many of the pages of this volume; perhaps S. M. (Carleton's pseudonym) may publish the story at length, in another shape" (*CE*, 11:945). Lack of space, however, was not the reason for cutting Carleton's manuscript, which ran for a total of fifty-one pages in four issues, because Otway had previously published sixty-nine pages of "Father Butler" in five issues. There are great differences between happy Dennis and melancholy James Butler. Dennis, a lively literary character who relives episodes of Carleton's youth during the period when he was planning to enter the seminary, does not convert to Protestantism. That is the major difference.

The story in the *Christian Examiner* is unlike the longer tale that appears in *Traits and Stories* (1833). In the journal, Dennis, old Dennis's son, is an ignorant country boy whose stupidity leads him into argumentative sessions with countrymen more ignorant than he. Before Dennis is accepted at the seminary, he assumes the dress, character, and manners of a parish priest and requests better food, a knife and fork, and a more formal relationship with his family. Father, mother, brothers, and sisters must call him "sir" and recognize his great talents as well as his new name, Dionysius, which befits a classical scholar. His proud parents grant his requests because they do not want to upset his delicate nature and intellectual pursuits, which distinguish him from their other twelve children. His mother is particularly proud of Dennis whose gentility, she believes, comes from her family, the Magennises, who are now regaining their former high social position through Dennis. She overrules the other children's objections to Dennis's demands by assuring them that following the ordination he will more than compensate for their sacrifices.

After asserting the rights and privileges due a man destined for the priesthood, Dennis visits with Father Finnerty about getting the bishop's approval of his candidacy. The priest informs Dennis who informs his father that the gift of a young colt to Father Finnerty will be a great help in receiving approval. He gets the colt, but Dennis is rejected because the bishop wants the colt. The entire family, neighbors, and relatives gathered to celebrate Dennis's acceptance at the seminary in Maynooth are astounded by the news. Eventually, Father Finnerty returns the colt, pleases the bishop, and gets Dennis accepted. The tale ends in the journal with Dennis walking away from his home toward his destiny at Maynooth.[8]

Evaluation of the *Christian Examiner* Contributions

Of the thirteen stories, four revised tales—"A Pilgrimage to Patrick's Purgatory," "The Station," "The Lianhan Shee," and "Dennis O'Shaughnessy Going to Maynooth"—became part of the *Traits and Stories.* Of these, "A Pilgrimage to Patrick's Purgatory" and "Dennis O'Shaughnessy Going to Maynooth" merit the highest critical praise. Otway, of course, had not intended it, but because of Carleton's writings in an anti-Catholic Protestant publication, more information about social conditions, family life, and Catholic practices in rural nineteenth-century Ireland is now known than would otherwise have been possible. The hundreds of characters introduced in these stories present a panoramic view of prefamine Ireland.

Carleton's descriptive skill places these people in their naturally beautiful countryside in stormy and peaceful days which means that his characters are not searching for place or identity. They are firmly established in their mud hovels, roadside hedge schools, earth-floored cabins, and open fields which serve as their cathedrals. With a unity of person and place, the stories assume a literary importance that transcend the purpose for which they were originally written. The revisions freed Carleton from Otway's influence. The author was anxious to present the religious practices and beliefs in "The Station" and "The Lianhan Shee" from an artist's viewpoint, and, above all, he wanted his own portraits in "A Pilgrimage to Patrick's Purgatory" and "Dennis O'Shaughnessy Going to Maynooth" to be true pictures of himself.

Unquestionably, Carleton developed writing skills under Otway's guidance, and their mutually profitable association continued until the artist decided to assert his independence. Carleton no longer wished to be an anonymous contributor. The first story was signed "W", and the next eleven bore "Wilton's" signature. In the final story, he was "S. M.", a minor writer among Otway's contributors. Their partnership ceased when Carleton acquired the confidence to express himself from an artistic perspective, but ironically the confidence was gained from his friendship with Otway who rejected the artistic viewpoint. At the time of the breakup, Carleton was a thirty-seven-year-old looking for another adventure, believing he could safely challenge Otway's editorial policy. Although Carleton was unsuccessful and ended his association on a discordant note, he owed much to Otway, because through him, Carleton had met people and publishers who could further his career. Characteristically, when he moved on, he had no money or job. His next major publication, *Traits and Stories,* second series, did not appear until 1833.

Chapter Three
Traits and Stories and *Tales and Sketches*

Traits and Stories, First Series

While Carleton was contributing to the *Christian Examiner,* he published "Dick Magrath, a Sketch of Living Character" (1829) in the *Dublin Family Magazine,* recording experiences of a hedge schoolmaster, which he later greatly expanded in "Denis O'Shaughnessy" and "The Poor Scholar." By writing four pages of "Confessions of a Reformed Ribbonman" (1830) and five pages of "The Three Tasks" (1830) for the *Dublin Literary Gazette,* Carleton was developing other ideas which became part of his fictional stock of tales. For the short-lived *National Magazine,* he wrote "The Donagh or Horse Stealers" (1830), "Alley Sheridan or The Runaway Marriage" (1830), "Laying a Ghost" (1831), and "The Landlord and Tenant" (1831), which dramatize incidents from the rural Irish culture. Without the restriction of meeting Otway's purpose, Carleton more naturally exposed the vice and virtue of his people in these short tales published as he simultaneously continued to write for the *Christian Examiner.*

Folk beliefs, legends, ghost stories, social customs, and the corrupt land system were discussed from Carleton's perspective, and he did not have to check his sympathy for the characters or involve them in religious controversy. He could also experiment with form, content, and organization for his first collection of eight short stories, *Traits and Stories of the Irish Peasantry,* first series (1830). The title for such a collection had already been suggested in the *Christian Examiner* where "The Station" and "The Brothers" were introduced under the supratitle, "Sketches of the Irish Peasantry."

In many ways, the term *peasantry* is an unfortunate one for it does not identify the actual nature of Carleton's fictional characters. Most of Carleton's literary characters are farmers who are leasing land, which sometimes has been in their family's possession for several generations. The men must bargain for their leases and compete against other farmers who can outbid them. Because of the Orange Lodges and Ribbon Societies, violence is part of the leasing system. These farmers with their wives and children, leading complicated lives, constitute a class of people who value education and retain their own literary traditions. Often, their ancestors owned the land being leased to them. Consequently, *peasantry* with its connotations of uncouthness and ignorance was a derogatory term for identifying that large and varied group of rural people.[1] Another term, *country people,* better describes the class. Since Carleton was still contributing to the anti-Catholic journal where the term *peasantry* originated, the stories were published under that title.

When considering the titles of the eight stories that appear in the first series of *Traits and Stories*—"Ned M'Keown," "The Three Tasks," "Shane Fadh's Wedding," "Larry M'Farland's Wake," "The Battle of the Factions," "The Pary Fight and Funeral," "The Hedge School," and "The Station"—it is apparent that they reveal a broad spectrum of Irish life. In this collection, there is also an attempt to organize the tales after Chaucer's *Canterbury Tales,* but adapted to the environment of nineteenth-century rural Ireland.

In "Ned M'Keown," the characters, each of whom is to tell a tale, sit around Ned's fireplace in what is definitely not a peasant's hut. The characters are not peasants, either, but represent the clergy and tradesmen. The house is a long white-washed building with a thatched roof, connected to a barn and situated in Carleton's Clogher Valley at the foothills of Knockmany Mountain. The house serves as a general store for the community. Ned is the proprietor, but he is continually harassed by his wife Nancy who is really the better business person.

The other characters are Andy Morrow, a respectable educated farmer; Bob Gott, a returned soldier; Tom M'Roarkin, an asthmatic storyteller; Bill M'Kinny, a poacher and jockey; Alick M'Kinley, a "farmer of substance"; Shane Fadh, teller of fairy tales and traditions; and Pat Frayne, a schoolmaster. The names are not fictitious but belong to people from County Tyrone that Carleton knew from his boyhood. Their activities and character sketches are also based on their actions and personalities.[2] A strange character who appears riding a black horse called Satan enters the house as the group is chatting about the ghost of a dead squire who is supposed to be haunting his old home. He is followed by Father Ned Deleery and his curate Father Peter M'Clatchaghan who soon begin to argue about Latin passages. They jokingly tell Andy Morrow that it is a shame he will be going to hell because he is Protestant. The remark is taken in good humor, and the relaxed men are ready to listen to Ned's story. The whiskey bottle passes freely from one to another on the stormy night at the house set by the crossroads of Kilrudden.

Ned's tale is "The Three Tasks" which is a mixture of folktales and local legends with a central figure, Jack Magennis, who on a frosty midnight walk meets a talking dog and a dark-looking man. Jack plays cards with the man and loses a bet which would have given him a bag of gold. Within a year, he must serve the man in his castle for a year and a day. The dog comes then with a green ribbon and a spyglass around his neck and a pair of Wellington boots on his hind legs. At the castle, Jack is given three impossible tasks: the cleaning of a stable that had not been cleaned in seven years, the catching of a wild filly, and the robbing, without the use of a boat or oar, of a crane's nest on the top of a tree in the middle of an island. Jack accomplishes the tasks because a beautiful young woman with magic powers helps him. She and Jack fall in love, escape from the castle, and return to Ireland where they bury enough money to make Jack a rich man. Just as he is to marry the beauty, his mother awakens him from the dream, which seems so real to Jack that he looks for the buried money. He finds it, and that, says Ned, accounts for the wealth of the Magennisses.

The tale is a good example of the universal folktale, revitalized for a particular Irish community. It was a rare type of tale for Carleton because he did not retell many of his father's legends and folktales or his own stories composed during his wandering days on his journey to Dublin. The impact of the witty "The Three Tasks" in which Carleton portrayed Ned's weak character is told in a footnote. Ned, Carleton says, "was certainly a very remarkable individual and became, in consequence of his appearance in these pages, a person of considerable notoriety during the latter years of his life" (*W*, 2:683). The author also confessed that Ned's henpecked character is inaccurate; he earned the sketch because Carleton was repaying Ned's past unkindness to him. After the tale is told, the guests depart and so does the stranger whose role in the story is not developed.

On the next night when the men gather around Ned's fireplace, Shane Fadh tells the story of his own wedding in "Shane Fadh's Wedding." The group, Carleton informs us, is composed of people with different religious principles and political beliefs living harmoniously together unlike the "rancorous spirit of the present day" (*W*, 2:683). Shane, whose wife has died a year ago, is remembering their marriage which took place decades earlier, but Carleton is writing of his brother's marriage and records the customs honored and expected by the couple and their families on such an occasion. It is a riotous rendering from the time fifteen barrels of whiskey are ordered to the dancing that goes on until after daybreak on the next day. Some of the choicest scenes describe the mounted wedding party heading for the priest's residence, the bachelors riding for the whiskey bottle at the home of the bridegroom, and the dinner with "lashins of corned beef, and rounds of beef, and legs of mutton, and bacon-turkeys and geese, and barn-door fowls, young and fat" (*W*, 2:696). Squire Whitehorn, the resident Protestant landlord, is also at the wedding and congratulates the couple who will be working on his estate secure in the knowledge that he will not evict them for Protestant tenants.

"Shane Fadh's Wedding," a joyous tale, tells of the industrious people who find their future linked to farming in Clogher Valley. The richness of Shane's characterization derives from the peculiarities of his language which transmit the feelings of his family at his marriage. It is customary at this time to ask for parents' forgiveness for past disobediences and to request their blessing. Shane tells of his mother's asking forgiveness if she has been too harsh on him: "'Oh, Shane Fadh—Shane Fadh, acushla machree [pulse of my heart]!' says my poor mother in

Irish, 'you're going to break up the ring around your father's hearth and mine—going to lave us, avourneen, [darling] for ever, and we to hear your light foot and sweet voice, morning, noon, and night, no more!'" (W, 2:689).

The unity of the tale comes from Shane Fadh's steady voice retelling the important event in his life with frequent transitional remarks about characters who have since died or left the region explaining why such events take place. In referring to the blessed candle his mother gives him to prevent a sudden death or accident, Shane Fadh describes it as an act of love which a mother performs when her child travels. Carleton presents the incident differently from the biased way in which the candle is handled in "Lachlin Murray and the Blessed Candle." In a footnote, he informs his readers that on Ash Wednesday the priest blesses a number of small wax candles for the people to wear until the following year (W, 2:690). This information reinforces Carleton's benign approach to the tale since the religious practices are not condemned, and the realistic characters are truly likable.

On the succeeding evening, it is wheezy M'Roarkin's turn to tell a story, and he coughs his way through "Larry M'Farland's Wake." It narrates the tale of Larry and Sally M'Farland, two disreputable characters of the parish. They complain about each other's shortcomings, neglect their work, and abuse their children. When Larry beats his son, his mother makes him drunk to overcome his pain. The hard picture of this family is softened by sympathy being generated for Larry who, on the night before he is to deliver oats to a mountain still, calls his family together and asks for forgiveness, especially from the beaten son. "Dick, come over to me, agra [love]," the father says, "Dick, come and sit down beside me. . . . I'm sorry for what I done to you last night . . . for I think that my heart is breaking" (W, 2:711). Sally and the children forgive Larry, and he goes off on his illegal mission in a howling storm. During the night Sally hears a banshee (woman of the fairies), and Larry's brother sees his fetch (a spirit that assumes the likeness of an individual and that, if seen after dark, means the immediate death of the person). Fulfilling the prophesies, drunken Larry drowns in a bog hole, and his pregnant wife on seeing his corpse goes into labor and dies. A noisy wake follows where there is no holding back the crowd of young men and women from playing the games associated with wakes, because no offense can be given to the corpses of disreputable people. Carleton describes several games, making "Larry M'Farland's Wake" a reliable source of social customs attached to wakes.

The story also describes the better nature of Larry's brother Tom and his wife who comfortably make a living without resorting to the sale of oats to a still. They pay for the costs of the wake, adopt the youngest children, and work harder to fulfill their added obligations. "Larry M'Farland's Wake" contrasts with "The Brothers" in the *Christian Examiner* in which Ned the Catholic brother is evil, stupid, and irreligious while Protestant Thomas is good, clever, and religious. Both stories were published in the same year and give some idea of Carleton's divided loyalty in continuing to contribute to Otway's journal.

In Carleton's defense, it must be said that he accepted Otway's judgments with reservations. Critics who condemn Carleton for his early contributions to the *Christian Examiner* also praise him for his early *Traits and Stories*. Therein lies the paradox in trying to evaluate his work in terms of development, because "The Brothers" and "Larry M'Farland's Wake" stand in the way of anyone who argues for an organic growth in Carleton's fiction.

"The Battle of the Factions," the next story in the series, is told on the next night. It recounts the knockdown, drag-out fight between the O'Hallaghans and the O'Callaghans who are hereditary enemies. Their animosity subsides long enough for Rose O'Hallaghan and John O'Callaghan to become engaged. But a great battle between their families occurs a week before their planned wedding, for the ill feelings between the two families are too much a part of their lives to be cast aside for the young couple. Even their landlords are involved with their battles and fight a duel to settle a dispute about land ownership for the O'Hallaghans and O'Callaghans. Curiously enough, although the families are renters, they consider themselves owners because for centuries their ancestors had originally owned the land. But neither landlords nor lawyers are able to stop the faction fighting, and a bitter fight takes place in which John O'Callaghan is slain in an unfair encounter with the brother of Rose O'Hallaghan. He cuts open the artery of John's neck with a scythe, and it is dreadful to see the blood gurgling and bubbling out, "ending in small red spouts, blackening and blackening, until they became fainter and more faint" (*W*, 2:740). Rose, who sees her lover killed, takes up a large stone in her apron and kills the assailant, not knowing he is her brother because he is covered with blood and dust.

The schoolmaster tells his audience that he is "not bright, however, at oral relation. I have accordingly composed into narrative the following tale, which is appellated 'The Battle of the Factions'" (*W*, 2:722). The tale is told by the grandson of Connor O'Callaghan with his biased portraits of the O'Halla-ghans who could not be at peace with a saint. Notable descriptions of the cudgels, characters of the fighters, and the tranquil scenery where the fighting occurs are given. One particular character, little Neal Malone who is the O'Callaghan's tailor (tradesmen must also fight for their faction), is a comic hero who fights against big Frank Farrell, the O'Hallaghan's miller. Neal protects himself from the miller's blows by jumping on his back and pelting his face and eyes with clinched fists, temporari-ly blinding his huge opponent. Neal becomes the comic hero of his own story in "Neal Malone" (1833), which is incorporated into *Traits and Stories* (1843–44).

With the schoolmaster's break in the proposed method of storytelling, the idea of the group continuing to meet for this purpose is abandoned. At the end of "The Battle of the Factions," Carleton says in a parenthetical statement that the original intention of every man telling a tale that illustrates Irish life, feelings, and manners was abandoned because it limited his work and the reader may tire of the excessive Irish dialogue and peculiar phraseology. He is now allowing "himself more room for description and observation" (*W*, 2:740).

"The Party Fight and Funeral" is the next story. The faction fight in comparison is a petty one because the party fight involves over four thousand men from the Orange Lodges and the Ribbon Societies in Counties Monaghan, Cavan, Ferman-agh, and Derry. Carleton here is narrating a scene he witnessed in Clogher when religious and political sentiments divided the populace into warring segments on a grand scale. A careful reading of the tale reveals that the nineteenth-century attitudes and traditional enmity has been passed on to contemporary battling Orangemen and provisional members of the Irish Republican Army (IRA). Carleton at that time documents the communal warfare that his generation inherited from the time of the Battle of the Boyne (1690)[3] and dramatizes the episodes by focusing upon one fighter, Denis Kelly. He educates his son Lanty to be a faction fighter against the Caseys and a party fighter against the Orangemen. Young Lanty assures his father he will beat the Caseys with his blackthorn stick and kill all the Orangemen. To which Denis replies, "That's my stout man, my brave little soger! Wus dha lamh avick!—give me your hand, my son!" (*W*, 2:771). Denis's wife does not share his beliefs and he ignores her efforts to make him give up fighting. He says, "I know it's wrong, but what can I do? Would you have me for to show the Garran-bane?" (white horse, symbolizing cowardice; James II escaped from the Battle of Boyne on a white horse) (*W*, 2:773).

The savage sectarian violence on the day of the great fight is described in much detail and centers on the hand-to-hand combat between Denis Kelly and John Grimes in which Kelly is fatally injured. He dies months after the fight, and his funeral almost ignites the fiery Orangemen and Ribbonmen into another battle but for the priest and Protestant landlord's intervention. This story presents Carleton's opposition to violence in Irish society, whether it is practiced by Orangemen or Ribbonmen. With the exception of *Valentine M'Clutchy,* he maintains this position in further works on the subject. In "The Party Fight and Funeral," Carleton appeals to the common sense and Christian understanding of the people to refrain from violence in settling their differences, and the gruesome vision of battered skulls, broken bones, and bloody bodies that he sketches is meant to evoke feeling against the senseless slaughter. The realistic picture is not simply a literary prop to shock readers; it is Carleton's judgment about the barbarism of Catholic and Protestant behavior in resolving conflict. Much of the impetus for such behavior, Carleton believes, is derived from the educational system, which he describes in the next tale, "The Hedge School."

The story corrects the misconception that country people were indifferent to education; as Carleton states, "The lower orders of no country ever manifested such a positive inclination for literary acquirements . . . and zeal for book learning" (*W*, 2:819). He narrates episodes in the life of Mat Kavanaugh, a schoolmaster, who replaced a schoolmaster who died of poverty and another who was hanged for burning the house of a land agent. Mat's adventures begin with his abduction by the men of Findramore who have not been able to attract a teacher to their town. Because Mat is well-treated, he stays on after advertising the scope of his teaching skills, which range from spelling, reading, writing, arithmetic, geometry, moral philosophy, and mythology to the classical studies of Ovid, "Cholera Morbus," and the "Greek Diagamma Resolved."

If the students learn slowly, Mat physically punishes them. However, his cruelty does not equal that practiced by some drunken teachers who lash their students' legs with branches, knock them down with their fists, hit them over the head with a cudgel, kick their shins with iron-nailed shoes, and whip their backs for minor behavioral problems or no offense at all. Although he presents a vivid account of typical school days by recording a series of sharp conversations between Mat and his students, Carleton is more interested in rendering an accurate picture of Mat's degenerate character. As a Ribbonman, Mat is involved with crimes committed at night against landlords and working tenants. He is finally caught, and his hanging is about to take place, but a last-minute appeal is granted when Mat betrays his companions. He calls himself a "Profissor of Humanities" and leaves Findramore before suffering the fate of an informer like that which befalls Barny Brady; he is found dead with a note in his mouth reading, "This is the fate of all informers."

Carleton in one of his frequent authorial intrusions wonders if ignorance is not better than the immoral and irreligious education given to the young, who then grow up and commit cruel crimes sanctioned by their teachers. They stimulate the children's minds by teaching inflammatory political matter which extolls the deeds of Irish rogues. These schoolmasters, Carleton notes, ridicule the Protestant church and predict its fall along with the rise of the Catholic church. "The Hedge School" does not complement the more tolerant tone of the other stories in the first series of *Traits and Stories,* which blame both Catholic and Protestant lifestyles for the continuous agrarian violence and social unrest. This story may have been destined for the *Christian Examiner* because it adheres to Otway's editorial policy, though sympathy is evoked for the battered students of the hedge schoolmaster. The better scenes are those describing Mat's abduction and his sessions with his captive students. They suffer the chaotic educational system of early nineteenth-century Ireland when neither the church nor the state assumed responsibility for educating the youth.

The concluding story is "The Station," which is, of course, the revised version of the story from the *Christian Examiner*. In this version, numerous footnotes are added explaining various religious and social practices, including the use of oatmeal by people who cannot afford to buy soap. Because of the explanatory notes and deletions of the overtly anti-Catholic passages, the revision achieves a measure of success that arises in part from the counterplay between Father Philemy M'Guirk and his parishioner, Phaddhy Sheemus Phaddhy. A new ending also accounts for the enduring fame of "The Station," which in *Traits and Stories* sketches the intimate relationship between the priest and his followers among the moral country people. In the new conclusion, Father M'Guirk is fatigued by the strenuous activities of the day. His condition alarms Phaddy's wife who sees that two men accompany the priest home. The story has few of the faults that weaken Carleton's fiction and many of the qualities that raise his stories above the level of mediocrity. M'Guirk is a credible heroic figure who functions as the central character in the community.

The critical reception to *Traits and Stories* was overwhelmingly favorable, and Carleton finally established a literary reputation. In Edinburgh, John Wilson, writing for *Blackwood's Magazine* under the pseudonym of Christopher North, says, "The whole book has the brogue. . . . never were the outrageous whimsicalities of that strange, wild, imaginative people so characteristically displayed; nor . . . is there any dearth of poetry, pathos, and passion."[4] Critics in London and Dublin also praised Carleton's real literary debut and recognized that a talent different from that of John and Michael Banim and Gerald Griffin had arrived on the scene.[5] Within three years, pirated editions of *Traits and Stories*, first series, were published in Philadelphia and Baltimore, which gives an idea of Carleton's popularity among the Irish emigrants. The American editions, for which Carleton received no royalty, also included a preface in which he states his intention in writing of his people. "The author . . . has endeavored to give his portraits as true to nature as possible neither to distort his countrymen into demons nor to enshrine them as suffering innocents and saints."[6]

Traits and Stories, Second Series

Following his success with *Traits and Stories,* Carleton contributed tales to the magazines being published in Dublin. "Neal Malone" (1833) and "The Dream of a Broken Heart" (1833) appeared in the *Dublin University Review and Quarterly* and "The Dead Boxer" (1833) in the *Dublin University Magazine.* To capitalize on the success of the first series, another edition of *Traits and Stories,* second series (1833), was published; it consists of ten stories, two of them revised from the *Christian Examiner:* "The Lianhan Shee" and "Denis O'Shaughnessy."

This set continues with the same characterization and presentation. Writing from an omniscient point of view, Carleton is the great storyteller, narrating events he has witnessed or experienced in rural Ireland. In these narrations his Rabelaisian humor plays a prominent role, and this quality which is suppressed in the *Christian Examiner* becomes a permanent part of his work. Four of the ten stories in the second series are conspicuously funny: "Phil Purcel the Pig Driver," "An Essay on Irish Swearing or The Geography of an Irish Oath," "Denis O'Shaughnessy," and "Phelim O'Toole's Courtship." The other six stories range from serious to somber to tragic: "The Midnight Mass," "The Donagh or The Horse Stealers," "The Lianhan Shee," "The Poor Scholar," "Wildgoose Lodge," and "Tubber Derg or The Red Well." It is not necessary to analyze each story to illustrate Carleton's superior skill in storytelling; the explication of one tale from each category will suffice.

"Phelim O'Toole's Courtship" is one of those stories that does not lose its appeal on rereading, because each time another nuance is detected in the characters or another quirk is discovered in their behavior. The main character is Phelim O'Toole, the only child of Larry and Sheelah O'Toole who have been married for almost seven years prior to his birth. With tongue in cheek, Carleton describes how Larry is sad from morning to night and Sheelah is sad from night to morning because they are childless. Larry weeps because he has no son to inherit the half acre that his father Tyrrell O'Toole passed on to him, and Sheelah weeps because she has no *pastiah* (child) at the hearth.

When not weeping, they curse each other for their misfortune until a *boccagh* (beggar) convinces them to go on a pilgrimage to a holy well. There, they are to pray, kiss the lucky stone of the well, circle it nine times, leave a ribbon or part of their dress, dance a bit with the other pilgrims, and come home, trusting to the holy saint to honor their request.[7] After complying with every rite, within a year Phelim, named after the patron saint of the lucky stone, is born, and he is the wonder of the neighborhood. Like a poet, Carleton says, Phelim is acquainted with the elements: "Wind and rain were his brothers, and frost also distantly related to him. With mud he was hand and glove, and not a bog in the parish, or a quagmire in the neighborhood, but sprung up under Phelim's tread" (*W*, 2:1038). The ironic metaphorical description adds to Phelim's charismatic characterization.

In describing his clothing, Carleton pictures Phelim as a moulting fowl with a few feathers, running before a gale in the barnyard. He is a wild unmanageable boy who takes advantage of his parents' love to speak, think, and behave as he wishes. The youngster lies and swears, assumes he is a minor deity, and steals whatever he wants from the neighbors. Unfortunately, Phelim contracts smallpox, despite Sheelah's folk preventive remedies which include the swinging of her son in the name of the Trinity three times over and under the body of an ass. On recovery, his face becomes scarred and one eye droops. His parents think he wears the pockmarks well, and Sheelah believes the drooping eye "makes him look so cunnin' an' ginteel, that one can't help havin' their heart fixed upon him" (*W*, 2:1042).

After delineating the character and physical appearance of Phelim at whom the girls laugh before he speaks, Carleton reintroduces Larry's concern about the inheritance of the half acre; this culminates in Phelim's courtship. In a series of ludicrous events, Phelim is engaged to three women: Bridget Doran, the priest's aged housekeeper; Peggy Donovan, a farmer's daughter; and Sally Flattery, the daughter of Phelim's cohort in crime. The banns of matrimony are announced at mass for Phelim and the three women, after which the women, their families, and friends converge on the half acre to denounce Phelim's deception. Phelim escapes from this escapade only to be trapped by Fool Art, the local idiot. The suitor is jailed for Ribbonism activities and transported for life; that is, he is exiled from Ireland. His parents, realizing their errors in educating the "bouncing" Phelim, become despondent. Larry drinks, neglects his work, and loses the half acre. He and Sheelah must then beg for their livelihood.

The reader may have difficulty in evaluating the justice of this conclusion, because of the comic characterization of the "hero" and the sympathy he evokes throughout the tale by his merry-making at fairs, dances, and social functions. Carleton makes the reader laugh at Phelim who has a simple relationship with the other characters, and it does not seem fair to abruptly change the reader's response to Phelim's absurdities. Except for that limitation, "Phelim O'Toole's Courtship" is a great comic tale. It exposes superstitious beliefs, folk medicine, and Christian rites mixed with pagan Irish ritual in a rural Irish community. Racy dialogues among the parents, Phelim, and his three women quickly move the story on to its unexpected ending. The many excellent descriptive passages add the finishing touches to the story, which holds a high place in the Carleton hierarchy of fiction.

"The Donagh" (*Domhnach,* something holy) is a powerful story that originally appeared in the *National Magazine.* It is a highly emotional tale, tightly structured, which revolves around an ancient relic and its effect upon the people. The main character is Anthony Meehan, a prototype of Donnel Dhu in *The Black Prophet* (1847), who hates society but loves his daughter Anne. Meehan is a thief who is beyond the law and the Catholic clergy. He dominates his younger brother Denny to the extent that Denny is often paralyzed with fear in Tony's presence. The Meehans are strangers in Carnmore, and their entry into the village is soon followed by the loss of sheep, cows, and horses. When the Cassidys lose a horse worth more than eighty guineas, the whole parish is in an uproar which subsides with the organization of a ceremony wherein suspected men swear their innocence on a Bible. Since it is the law, or Protestant Bible, the Meehans, who have stolen the horse, falsely swear without fear or hesitation.

However, the Cassidys, the magistrate, and Father Farrell demand that the suspects also swear on the Donagh, an ancient relic consisting of a wooden box plated with silver and believed at one time to have housed the gospel of St. Patrick. Sudden death, madness, suicide, paralysis, or some other catastrophic calamity would follow perjury upon the Donagh, which explains the awe and astonishment that comes over the crowd when Father Farrell calls the suspects before him. Anthony moves forward, but Denny is rooted to the ground and passes out on seeing Anthony kiss the Donagh avowing his innocence. A hush arises from the excited crowd which thinks that Denny has perjured himself and dropped dead. Within minutes, however, he revives, and Anthony who is sneering at him because of his cowardice forces him up to kiss the Donagh. In terror, Denny, who is more afraid of the relic than of his brother, confesses. This enrages Anthony. He is about to shoot Denny, but Anne restrains him and is killed by the bullet intended for her uncle. Shocked and shaken, Meehan begs Anne's forgiveness: "Oh! I'm far cowlder now! Tell me that you forgive me, acushla oge machree! Manim asthee hu [Young pulse of my heart! My soul is within thee], darlin' say it" (*W*, 2:899). She dies not forgiving him. Tony cries out in anguish, topples over, and dies beside his daughter.

The tale demonstrates the force of religious ritual and its importance in Irish society. Joseph Campbell believes that ritual functions to "give form to human life, not in the way of a mere surface arrangement, but in depth."[8] Carleton understood the depth of his culture's commitment to the religious rituals that bound it together, because during his early life these rituals and social customs fastened him to that culture. When he wrote about those experiences, he did so from well within the heart of his people. "The Donagh" illustrates Carleton's intimate association with the culture he was observing.

Carleton said that the story brought to light the curious nature of the relic and the difference of opinions about its age as expressed by Reverend Dr. O'Beirne, headmaster of the school of Portora at Enniskillen, and Sir William Bethan, an Irish antiquarian. He reprinted all their letters to him which disclose a profound interest in the relic and its role in centuries of Irish history. The author also recorded the opinion of another antiquarian, George Petrie, who, as a member of the Royal Irish Academy, sketched the Donagh and lectured about it before the academy. He stated that this relic and indeed all the ancient relics were venerated only in association with the original church to which they belonged. Petrie said that Carleton's "The Donagh" was a "recent popular tale of great power . . . in which the superstitious uses to which this reliquary has long been applied, are ably exhibited, and made subservient to the interests of the story" (*W*, 2:903). The story and others like it convey the sense of place that was so highly developed in Ireland where an individual belonged to a locality and adhered to the traditions of the area because of binding unwritten laws.

Other Editions of *Traits and Stories*

The eighteen stories that constitute the first and second series of *Traits and Stories* are not the complete collection published under that title; a new edition of *Traits and Stories* (1843–44) includes the eighteen tales and two others, "The Lough Derg Pilgrim" and "Neal Malone." Both of them have been included in subsequent editions and are a permanent part of the collection. The plot and the significance of "The Lough Derg Pilgrim" (the revised version of "A Pilgrimage to Patrick's Purgatory") have already been discussed. An explication of "Neal Malone" reveals that it belongs within the category of comic tales.

The satiric manner in which Carleton introduces Neal Malone, the great-souled tailor who, although only four feet in height, "paced the earth with the courage and confidence of a giant,"[9] endears him to the reader. Neal has an aggressive character and is frustrated because no one fights with him. "Am I never to get a bit of fightin'?" he calls out at a fair, "I'm blue-mowled for want of a batin'!"[10] He pleads in vain for a friend or enemy to fight with him, but his presence becomes a sign of peace. This induces a state of melancholy in Neal, affecting his health and his work. Determined finally to battle his shadow, Neal is defeated by nature which sends a cloud over the garden where the combat is to occur. Mr. O'Connor, the schoolmaster, offers Neal advice to cure his melancholy. He is to marry and discover the life of continual warfare that O'Connor is experiencing.

Neal happily falls in love with women in general and decides to find someone to suit his feelings. O'Connor suggests the butcher's daughter, Biddy Neil, believing she will fulfill Neal's "Universal Passion," a rare emotional state. Biddy Neil is twice Neal's size and has three times his strength, which is why O'Connor thinks she is the ideal woman, reasoning that large animals are placid. The wedding takes place, and within four months Neal is totally subdued; his wife refuses to allow him to attend fairs, visit his friends, or talk to other women in the village. Whereas formerly he walked the earth like a giant, he now puts weights in his pockets so the wind will not blow him off the earth.

Three unsuccessful suicide attempts attest to his nothingness: he has no blood to flow from his severed artery, no gravity to help him hang, no weight to help him sink under the waves. It is difficult to distinguish between Neal and his shadow or to hear his voice which becomes fainter and fainter until it is no more than a ringing in the ears. "Such was the awful fate of the tailor," Carleton writes, "who, as a hero, could not of course die; he merely dissolved like an icicle . . . and finally melted away beyond the perception of mortal sense."[11] The comic fable is a dramatic tall tale in which Neal's fate is decided by the gods who can see beyond the shadow and hear beyond the ringing in the ears.

"Neal Malone" is a unique tale because of the broad literary base upon which Neal's character is developed. Although he is a member of a rural community, he is not really a part of it despite the genealogical history that traces his ancestry through generations of fighting men back to the sixteenth century. Relationships between Neal and his neighbors are fanciful, and his character evolves against a background of classical references to his being a breech-maker to the gods and the tailor who cut Jupiter's winter clothes. In explaining Neal's transformation from a fighter to a lover, Carleton says it is not so unusual—look at Jack Falstaff or Ben Jonson.

Carleton attributes the former relative happiness of Neal to the contrasting unhappiness of O'Connor which cannot be understood unless the reader is "deeply read in modern novels."[12] Neal's siege of Biddy Neil, likened to Marshall Gerald's siege of Antwerp, and his illogical actions can only be understood by Locke or Dugald Stewart (the Scottish common sense philosopher and friend of Maria Edgeworth). Carleton puns on Neal's occupation by saying that he cannot "trace a principle—as what tailor, except Jeremy Taylor, could?"[13] The story is entirely enjoyable, humorous to the end (unlike "Phelim O'Toole"), and a lasting tribute to Carleton's comic sensibility.

Historically, the twenty tales identified in the editions of 1830, 1833, and 1843–44 comprise *Traits and Stories*. Any or all of them may be published under that title. However, sometimes stories that are not part of the origianl or expanded editions are published under that title, as is "Art Maguire or The Broken Pledge" which is listed under the title *Traits and Stories* in *The Works of William Carleton* (1970).

The tales' long publication history ensured the reputation of their author. He used them to express his personal prejudices about his early acquaintances, which he may have altered later after his temper cooled and the environment changed. *Traits and Stories* established his literary kingdom in Ulster and Meath, unlike that of Gerald Griffin whose collection of short stories in the *Holland-Tide* (1827) about middle-class family life off the Kerry coast sets his kingdom in the Munster province. Carleton's realm was different, too, from that of John and Michael Banim, coauthors of *The Tales of the O'Hara Family* (1825, 1827) set in Kilkenny. The collections by Griffin, the Banims, and Carleton are like ancient relics that acquire their value from being attached to a specific place before assuming a greater worth in the national treasury of Irish literature.

When one looks into the period from which *Traits and Stories* evolved, it is evident that a new and exciting form of Irish literature was beginning, which contained much of the spirit and tradition of ancient and medieval literature written in the Irish language. Certainly, Carleton's stories are transitional specimens, exhibiting a greater use of English to transmit the poetical and prosaic attitudes of the people. The frequent use of the Irish language, especially when the characters are under emotional stress, indicate that people were not confronting reality through only the English language.

Carleton's early short stories in a comprehensive context are significant because they reinforce the work of Griffin and the Banims. The combined works of these authors constitute a major category of Irish regional literature. According to Lucien Leclaire who evaluated this group of authors, "En fait l'un des auteurs les plus importants de cette periode—est William Carleton" (Actually, William Carleton is the most important of the authors of that period).[14] This critical acclaim is warranted because of the emotional intensity that Carletonian characters convey. More often than not, a mixed dramatic dialogue in English and Irish transfers their charged feelings to the reader. It is impossible, even for today's audiences, to read *Traits and Stories* without being moved to pity, compassion, laughter, or tears because of the vibrant personalities of the protagonists.

Tales and Sketches Illustrating the Character, Usages, Traditions, Sports and Pastimes of the Irish Peasantry

Carleton contributed more stories and some novels to the *Dublin University Magazine* from 1834 until 1860. Partly because of a quarrel with Charles Lever, an editor for the magazine,[15] Carleton published his many character sketches in the *Irish Penny Journal,* a cheap short-lived publication (1840-41) aimed at the working classes. This printing effort was patterened after the many inexpensive works being published in London for the working class in early Victorian urban England with "its distinct culture and literature."[16] Many working people in Dublin were displaced country people who enjoyed reading about the rural characters that Carleton sketches for the *Irish Penny Journal.* The stories emphasize individuals, and many of the characters are actual people who were part of a disappearing class of rural Ireland. Yet Carleton preserved their identity almost twenty years after associating with them. It is truly remarkable that he remembered so many details about these people in order to produce such pulsating portraits, an indication that authentic individuality is a prominent part of his literary realm. Carleton's particular social reality of prefamine rural Ireland with all its color, sounds, and actions depicts a totality of the situation that no other writer captures. His dramatic stories presented in the *Irish Penny Journal* were republished in James Duffy's *Tales and Sketches* (1845) during Carleton's nationalistic period. This work unlocks the doors of many Irish cabins and cottages.

Twenty-one stories were collected for *Tales and Sketches*, and they are generally of shorter length than the tales in *Traits and Stories*. "Rose Moan the Irish Mid-Wife," "Frank Finnegan the Foster-Brother," and "Mary Murray the Irish Match-Maker" represent the spirit of the character sketches in *Tales and Sketches*. It also contains legends, fairy tales, and sketches of other national types. The collection is dedicated to Sir Charles Gavan Duffy, an editor of the *Nation* and Carleton's lifetime friend. Duffy, according to Carleton, did more than any other man in such a short time to elevate the national mind and purify its taste. In the preface, the author assures the reader of the tales' authenticity and states they represent the simplicity of country life. "Rose Moan," capturing the unsophisticated nature of rural living, is a storehouse of information about this most important character. Before introducing her, Carleton writes of midwives in general and their attributes, which include both practical and fairy knowledge.

It is believed, for instance, that they know the secret of making beer from heather, which the Danish invaders of Ireland knew and transmitted to an Irish midwife who attended the birth of a Dane's child. The midwives also have the power, given by the fairies, to transfer the mother's pain to the father if he has ever abused the mother. In addition, midwives can cure the pangs of jealousy between spouses by concocting a special potion from herbs; they can interpret dreams and treat most sicknesses with folk remedies, charms, or incantations. When Rose is called to deliver Dandy Keho's baby, she comes in all this glory. Immediately, she inspects Mrs. Keho and sends a servant to the field for barley tops from which a paste is made and given to the mother to strengthen the uterine contractions.

Carleton notes that the paste is similar to ergot of rye (the source of ergotrate used by modern gynecologists for the same purpose). Rose does not leave immediately after the birth, but joins the family in toasting the new arrival. She returns for its christening a week later, adding safeguards to protect the infant from the fairies.

All births, however, are not happy events. Illegitimate births, although rare, cause special problems among the poor. The mother may not keep her child because of shame and poverty. The parish cares for the children; consequently, they are called *parisheens* and are nursed by foster mothers and reared as though they are blood relatives. "Frank Finnegan the Foster-Brother" tells the story of Frank, a parisheen, who grows up loved by the Hewson family that cares for him. His tale is set during the Irish Rebellion of 1798, when young Hewson is caught by the British who successfully quell the insurrection. Finnegan, his foster brother, helps Hewson escape but is captured in the process; he is offered a pardon if he will tell the magistrate of Hewson's whereabouts. Finnegan refuses, proudly telling the astonished judge that he will die happily in Hewson's place as Hewson would do the same for him. Later, Hewson slays the man responsible for Finnegan's death to avenge his execution by a firing squad. The tale relates the usual social violence and an unusual social custom associated with adopted children.

Women, besides assisting at births and nursing parisheens, also function as matchmakers. In the Irish language, such a woman is called a "Cosherer, a general negotiator in all such matters of love."[17] "Mary Murray the Irish Match-Maker" illustrates the particular talents of the matchmaker, a vital person in the domestic affairs of the country people. In this story, Mary Murray knows everyone and everything, traveling throughout the parish. Although she is disliked by couples whose unhappy marriages she arranged, she is welcomed everywhere because most of her matchmaking results in happy marriages. In narrating Mary's activities, which include knitting and quiltmaking for she is always busy, Carleton gives a good picture of domestic scenes in which ordinary events are taking place. The sketch, written well with Carleton's customary skill, describes minute details. Thus, "Mary Murray the Irish Match-Maker" is one of the many realistic tales that Carleton wrote of rural Ireland.

These three tales and the others in *Tales and Sketches* are like mirrors, reflecting diverse scenes of country life. The stories re-create a particular segment of a past culture to a perfection unequaled by other Irish writers of the period. In England, Dickens approaches Carleton's accomplishment, but no American writer presents such a complete picture of any segment of early nineteenth-century American society. Despite the literary accomplishment this collection of stories represents, Carleton is still a relatively unknown artist. When the initial impact of *Traits and Stories* derived from the conservative Protestants is added to the striking force of *Tales and Sketches* generated by the national Catholics, a powerful effect is produced which neither Protestant nor Catholic can diminish. Carleton's short stories established a sound reputation which his novels reinforced. If his literary output had ceased with the short fiction, the reputation would have continued.

Chapter Four
The Early Novels

Jane Sinclair and *Fardorougha the Miser*

No one disputes Carleton's mastery of the short story. His friends know him "as a writer of sketches without any particular beginning or end, as a painter of scenery, and as a narrator of a stirring event" (*L,* 2:34). He entered the novelist's arena with "Jane Sinclair or The Fawn of Springvale" (1836) which appeared serially in the *Dublin University Magazine.*

The attempt failed because the story is a misty romantic tale about middle-class Anglo-Irish Protestants. There is no central character, although it could (or should) have been Jane Sinclair whose unhappy love affair is being narrated. There are no vivid characters to redeem the wretched plot which is dull and sentimental. One wonders why an Irish countryman of Carleton's background attempted to describe a young lady's romantic life. If he was trying to break into the Victorian literary circle, Jane Sinclair is not the character to mark his point of entry. She is a poor Irish cousin to the Victorian heroines, and her unbelievable thoughts and actions result from the author's unfamiliarity with the emotional trauma of a rejected lady in love. Jane is mawkish and weeps through most of the tale, which not only does not move forward but weakens as it progresses. Because of the poor plot and unreal characterizations, *Jane Sinclair* is not one of Carleton's successful novels.

On the second attempt, he improved his characterization and subject matter by writing of a world with which he was intimately acquainted. The Tyrone native worked out the details of a common rural occurrence, described the action, created a magnificent central character, Fardorougha (dark Man), and structured a comprehensive plot to complement his characterization. "Faradorougha the Miser or The Convicts of Lisnamona" first appeared serially in the *Dublin University Magazine* from 1837–38 and was "ranked by his admirers among Carleton's foremost contributions to literature" (*L,* 2:35). It was printed by Curry as *Fardorougha the Miser or The Convicts of Lisnamona* (1839), followed by an American edition under the title of *The Miser or The Convicts of Lisnamona* (1840). By far, the greatest edition is *Feardorcha Truaillidhe* (Fardorougha the Miser) (1933), translated into Irish by Sean MacMaolain. The highly charged emotional conflicts and tender scenes are aptly expressed in the poetical Irish language.

Its instantaneous success and enduring critical praise results in part from the perceptive psychological portrait of the miser. Fardorougha O'Donovan is the central character who shines brightest in this galaxy of gregarious Irish Catholic country people; his co-star is his wife Honora. Their son Connor plays an outstanding role as the best supporting character.

In the preface to the fourth edition, Carleton says that Honora, a character study of his mother, represents the "pious women who have risen triumphant over some of the severest trials of domestic life."[1] Carleton was no longer looking at the women of the Protestant ascendancy for models, recognizing that literary merit rests on credible rather than upper-class characterization. Since the hollow characterizations in *Jane Sinclair* produced a weak novel, Carleton was forced back into the recesses of his own creativity until it shaped the solid characterizations of his strong people.[2] He built up tension between Fardorougha and Honora who face an epic struggle against social evils they neither cause nor control.

The novel tells the story of three Catholic families: Fardorougha, Honora, and Connor O'Donovan; Bodagh Buie (yellow churl) O'Brien, his wife Bridget, son John, and daughter Oonagh (Una); and Dan Flanagan, his wife, and four children. Fardorougha has a relatively secure hold upon his leased land because as he acquires money it is lent at usurious interest rates to his fellow farmers. He drives a hard bargain, always demands the money when due, and takes the collateral if money is not available. The miser subjects Honora and Connor to a Spartan existence and deprives them of everything but the barest essentials. They, unable to change his behavior, love him despite his handling of the household. Bodagh Buie, who is Michael O'Brien to his family and friends, is named after his father, a boorish farmer who acquires wealth by fair and foul means, which Bodagh Buie inherits. His uncultivated wife assumes an absurd vulgarity by acting like the landed gentry. Their gentle son John is a seminarian at Maynooth, and their beautiful daughter Una, the *colleen dhas dhun* (pretty dark-haired girl), loves Connor O'Donovan. Dan Flanagan is a small farmer unable to repay a loan to Fardorougha. He evicts the entire family which means the daughters must work as maids and the sons as laborers. Bartle Flanagan is the bitter son who works for O'Donovan, feigns friendship for Connor while planning his destruction, and loves Una O'Brien. The action arises from counterplays among the O'Donovans, O'Briens, and Bartle Flanagan with some help from the servants of O'Donovan and O'Brien and the men in the local Ribbon Society headed by Bartle Flanagan.

The opening dramatic scene, Connor's birth to the O'Donovans who were childless for fourteen years, discloses the conflict that plagues Fardorougha throughout his lifetime: his love of money and his love of Connor. Having been a notorious miser, O'Donovan uses his son as an excuse for his avarice because now he must save for his son's education and welfare. The O'Donovans live more poorly as the miser's greed becomes greater over the years. He is hated in the community to the same degree that Connor and Honora, who often assist Fardorougha's victims, are loved. Another moving scene, the miser's visit to O'Brien to arrange for Connor's marriage, demonstrates the conflict between his avarice and affection for his son. The O'Briens think Fardorougha is insane to propose such a union, because Connor is penniless since his father gave him nothing but the promise of an inheritance. The lovers are heartbroken, but their unhappiness is secondary to the grief that overcomes both families when Bartle Flanagan burns O'Brien's barn and frames Connor. He is arrested, and Fardorougha's intense agony almost kills him because he cannot part with the money to hire a group of lawyers for Connor's defense. They do not agree to the miser's condition, the tripling of their fees to be paid after his death, and he collapses from fright after thinking, "Wouldn't it be downright murdher in me to let him be lost if I could prevint it." (*W*, 1:242).

Fardorougha hires the lawyers only to discover that his banker has absconded with his funds. The miser is sure he will die like a dog in the ditch from starvation in addition to losing his son. Connor's defense, in the meanwhile, is paid by Una whose brother John handles the details. The lawyers are unsuccessful, and Connor is convicted and scheduled for execution. Several excellent scenes follow which illustrate Honora's unending faith in God's mercy and her anger at her husband's blasphemy. She, Fardorougha, and Una visit Connor in prison, and it is evident that Honora's spiritual strength keeps the family going until an appeal changes the sentence from execution to exile.

Fardorougha, somewhat reformed, sells everything so he and Honora can accompany Connor to New South Wales. To show their parental love, Carleton has them arguing about who has the better right to sleep in their son's bed during his imprisonment. The novel does not tell of the O'Donovans' sailing on the prison ship or their living for two years near Connor's penal colony; rather, the narrative follows Bartle Flanagan's relationship with the O'Briens and his attempt to abduct Una in a runaway marriage which is foiled by a servant. Flanagan is caught shortly after the aborted abduction in which he steals O'Brien's money and is sentenced to hang for his crimes. While awaiting execution, Flanagan confesses to Connor's alleged crime which brings the O'Donovans back to Ireland.

Carleton vividly describes Flanagan's execution, basing it upon an event that occurred four years earlier when a condemned man, shrieking with terror, had to be forced to the gallows. The author says, "There is nothing mentioned here which did not then occur, but there is much omitted" (W, 1:312). The O'Briens, reconciled to the marriage between Una and Connor, happily await his return. The joyous homecoming is saddened, however, by Fardorougha's dying condition. From his sick bed, he advises Connor not to love money too much but to save it nevertheless. Honora and Connor exchange melancholy glances when Fardorougha tells his son to drive a hard bargain and "never lind a penny o'money widout interest" (W, 1:316). Fardorougha, unaware that he is back in Ireland, struggles with thoughts of dying in a country where he will be buried in a strange grave, but he sees Connor and is comforted knowing they will sleep together. The inveterate miser dies in the arms of his wife and son. After a decent interval, Connor and Una marry and have sons and daughters who are loved by Honora and the O'Briens.

Fardorougha the Miser is to Carleton's novels what *Traits and Stories* is to his short stories in that the great novel sets a standard that subsequent novels may reach but never surpass. The excellent characterizations of the miser, his pious wife, and noble son are matched by the fine characterizations of "the wealthiest" Bodagh, "the proudest" Bridget O'Brien, and the "cowardly accomplished miscreant," Bartle Flanagan. The psychological nuances of the miser's conflict add a special excellence to his characterization which a contemporary reviewer in the *Athenaeum* thought was more realistic than Balzac's characterization of the miser Père Grandet in *Eugenie Grandet*.[3] Carleton's novel in a highly individual way voraciously uses his personal experiences to assimilate a wide range of material, whether from life or reports about life, and presents a unified tale of an agrarian Irish society in which Catholic Irishmen vie against each other. The characters act out the roles of actual farmers who lived with exorbitant interest rates, evictions, executions, and forced emigrations. O'Donovan's character represents the hardened individual who protects himself by destroying others. Neither he nor his neighbors, Carleton demonstrates, make any effort to correct injustices. Eventually, the external laws of the British system which the Irishmen do not understand determine their destiny. When the O'Briens learn to accept the O'Donovans on a moral rather than a financial basis, peace returns to the troubled community. This is proper to Carleton who saw the rural population, which constituted 80 percent of the Irish people, as the real Ireland.[4] The Flanagans who are productive and peaceful prior to O'Donovan's cruelty, however, represent the true victims in an immoral society. Dan Flanagan has no defense against O'Donovan, and Bartle's revenge is counterproductive. These realistic characterizations, pieced together from the memory of his mother, the Murphys in Lowtown, Ribbonmen, and a newspaper article about a hanged criminal, are excellent.

Because of his identification with the agrarian culture, the important question Carleton raises in *Fardorougha the Miser* is who shall inherit the land? The unequivocal response is that it shall be the virtuous Catholic man and woman whose sufferings prepare them for their inheritance. The Protestant magistrate administering laws that are foreign to the three Catholic families is an unsympathetic character who represents the government. Fardorougha cannot imagine that anyone would believe Connor is a criminal and tries to ignore the judicial power. Bodagh tells Una that it is the government and not he who is prosecuting her lover. Bartle, whose class bears the brunt of both Catholic and Protestant neglect, knows enough about the law to arrange damaging circumstantial evidence against Connor and to avoid detection by falling back upon the social justice of Ribbonism. It is only after Bartle violates and flaunts the Ribbon Society's ethical code that he is captured and punished by the British system. The complex relationships that develop within the corrupt Irish land system are dependent, of course, upon the nature of the landowner.[5] Carleton directs the reader's attention toward land leasers and owners of moderate holdings acquired by shrewd practices rather than toward landowners themselves. Enchanted by his earlier existence, he reproduces it powerfully with a joyful vision of the future. Carleton places Connor and Una in a prelapsarian Eden where the O'Donovan-O'Brien children will live a good life derived from secure land ownership.

Two conflict levels heighten the suspense in the novel; at the upper level, Carleton exposes the dominant social forces that pit man against man, and at the lower level, he dramatizes personal conflicts within a family and within an individual. His handling of the two types of conflicts differs from the manner in which conflicts are handled by Tom Moore in *Memoirs of Captain Rock* (1824), John and Michael Banim in *The Nowlans* (1826) and *The Mayor of Windgap* (1835), and Gerald Griffin in *The Collegians* (1829). These realistic Irish novels, which pre-date *Fardorougha the Miser,* are concerned with divergent social forces outside Carleton's ken and do not concentrate upon a man's obsession which tortures him and his family. Griffin's crazed lover, Hardress Cregan, most nearly suffers Fardorougha's psychological pain but without affecting the Cregan family. Carleton depicts the dominant social forces and the personal psychological conflicts in relationship to the land. His land-hungry characters record the workingmen's struggle to acquire land. Getting a lease and keeping it are problems of the landless who are firmly attached to the soil and act as though they own the land they farm.

The serious tone of *Fardorougha the Miser* accurately presents the conflicts troubling the country people. It contrasts with Charles Lever's early comic presentations of Irishmen who apparently have no problems in *The Confessions of Harry Lorrequer* (1839) and *Charles O'Malley* (1841) and Samuel Lover's *Rory O'More* (1836) and *Handy Andy* (1842). Carleton is part of the Irish realistic literary tradition that Maria Edgeworth, the "great Maria" as Sir Walter Scott calls her, established with *Castle Rackrent* (1800), *Ennui* (1809), *The Absentee* (1812), and *Ormond* (1817) wherein land ownership and the proper treatment of tenants by resident landlords play a major thematic role. Both the social and personal conflicts in *Fardorougha the Miser* arise from the corrupt land system that controls the entire rural population.

The strength of Carleton's novel rests on its emphasis of the tenants' intraclass conflicts as opposed to the power of Edgeworth's novels which was generated by landlords' conflicts. She reflects her family's landownership in Ireland and her struggles to keep Edgeworthstown after her brother, unlike her father, mortgages the estate by mismanagement.[6] Her well-educated characters love the luxuries of life, but Carleton's illiterate characters are unfamiliar with luxuries because they are too close to starvation. The prime motivation for Fardorougha's avarice is his fear of starvation; yet he subjects the Flanagans to that possibility by evicting them from their small landholding. Fardorougha is an archetypal miser with frequent mood changes involving severe depression, mania, hysteria, arrogance, love, and hate. He consistently inflicts pain upon members of his class. His recurrent nightmare of dying in a ditch with his throat scorching and his bones protruding from his skin is a sign that no one cares for his welfare. Other characters are equally stressed. Bartle Flanagan's thirst for vengeance is quenched when he harms Connor to get to Fardorougha, and Bodagh O'Brien's refusal to allow his daughter to have anything to do with Connor changes only after she almost dies from grief. Connor and Una are passive characters in the class struggle, hurt by their families. The novel was a black contribution to the fabric of Irish literature being created by Edgeworth,

Otway, Maturin, Moore, the Banim brothers, Griffin, Lever, and Lover. Carleton presented the history of his troubled people while commenting simultaneously upon intrapersonal and intraclass conflicts.[7]

To anyone not familiar with Irish history, it may seem strange that this novel discussed famine, agrarian violence, and class conflicts before the Famine of 1845. It was not a prophetic novel, however, because the conditions were recollections of scenes that Carleton witnessed following the end of the Napoleonic wars when the prices for grain and livestock tumbled. The early famines of 1817 and 1822, harbingers of the Great Famine, linked survival with the hardening of hearts to the least fortunate because the economy rewarded those with capital, regardless of their method of obtaining it. Both "the dark man" and the "yellow churl" represent two despised types of capitalists whose moral children, protected from the hostile environment by their manipulative fathers, restore a just social order. *Fardorougha the Miser* is a novel of manners which describes the differences among the social classes of rural Ireland. In *Valentine M'Clutchy*, on the other hand, Carleton tried to portray the manners, aspiration, and lifestyles of the landlord, his agent, and their tenants.

Valentine M'Clutchy

The first edition of *Valentine M'Clutchy the Irish Agent or The Chronicles of the Castle Cumber* (1845) with illustrations by Phiz was published in three volumes by James Duffy and marked Carleton's surge of nationalism springing from his association with Thomas Osborne Davis, Charles Gavan Duffy, and John Blake Dillon, cofounders of the *Nation*. Its editorial policy directly opposed the conservative *Christian Examiner* and *Dublin University Magazine*. The second edition in one volume with its ironic title, *Valentine M'Clutchy the Irish Agent or The Chronicles of Castle Cumber Together with the Pious Aspirations, Permissions, Vouchsafements, and other Sanctified Privileges of Solomon M'Slime, a Religious Attorney*, placed Carleton in his former enemy's camp where everyone did not welcome the infamous apostate. Some nationalists objected to the "writer of so many anti-Catholic productions being held up to the admiration of his countrymen" (*L,* 2:66). Objections were also forth-coming from the conservative periodical editors who generally attacked Carleton's perfidy. He explained his action in the preface by saying the novel presents "Irish life and manners that have never been given to the public before by any other writer upon the same subject."[8] To please the nationalists, the author admitted his early works were "not calculated to do any earthly good; but on the contrary, to give unnecessary offence to a great number of my countrymen."[9] The novel, according to the author, had two purposes: to shock landlords and agents to their proper duty and to teach the bigoted conservatives a lesson. He was "confident the Conservative Press of Ireland will not only sustain me but fight my battles, if I shall be ungener-ously attacked."[10]

The novel fulfilled Carleton's promise to the editors of the *Nation* who had asked for a serial tale, but they published it as a separate work to magnify its effect, causing Carleton to be identified with the Young Ireland movement. Although it has literary limitations, for Ireland the novel was a work that Benedict Kiely thinks "is the most important book of the nineteenth century."[11] Its plot, which dramatizes the evils of Protestant landowners, agents, clergy, and attorneys, made the book a significant contribution to the national cause. The young men and women striving to free Ireland after O'Connell's failure to mobilize enough support to repeal the Union Act needed Carleton's pen, and he used it for their political propaganda. In evaluating the novel, one has to keep in mind the purpose for which it was written and judge it accordingly. Since the theme is closer to history than fiction, the subject matter is realistic, but the characterizations of Valentine M'Clutchy and Solomon M'Slime are caricatures. These villains are stock characters without the individuality of the characters in the short stories or *Fardorougha the Miser.*

The plot was conceived for sociopolitical reasons, not unlike the plots in the *Christian Examiner* stories written for the opposite side. It exposed more violence, suffering, and misery than any of Carleton's previous tales. He placed bits and pieces of broken Ireland in the novel and miraculously assembled them at the conclusion to form a united Ireland where men and women of all classes and creeds live harmoniously together.

Valentine M'Clutchy is an optimistic novel of reform with a fairy-tale ending. It acquainted Englishmen with rural Ireland's problems not found in Thackeray's "The Irish Sketch Book" (1843), which was dedicated to Charles Lever, an antinationalist. Carleton understood that Thackeray "knew Ireland very well in an English way" (*L,* 2:156), but he did not know the violent effects of eviction laws upon a rural community. Valentine M'Clutchy, for instance, can evict an entire community by conniving with the local attorney Solomon M'Slime to legalize the evictions. The Orange police force brutally executes the eviction order because the laborers voted against their landlord in an election. The fraudulent process is easily accomplished, since the laws are simplified to allow an agent and an attorney to prejudicially evict tenants; other farmers willingly pay higher rents although they must starve themselves to do so.

Five families are involved in *Valentine M'Clutchy.* Valentine (an ironic name) is the illegitimate son of Squire Randal Deaker and Kate Clark; he has a son Philip. Hugh and Mary O'Regan have three sons, Ned, Brian, and Torley. Poll Doolin has one son Raymond-na-hatta (of the hat). Tom Topertoe, a "Union" lord, has two sons, Lord Cumber and Richard Topertoe. Brian and Kathleen M'Loughlin have three sons and a daughter Mary. These families interact with one another and with the Catholic and Protestant clergy characterized in the novel. The M'Clutchys and the Topertoes are Protestant; the others are Catholic. The success of the novel depends on the moral Catholic families fighting the immoral Protestant landlord and agent. Consequently, the major conflict is between the Protestant ascendancy and the Catholic tenantry, and the domestic or intraclass strife is minimal.

The story tells of the suffering tenants on the estate of Lord Cumber, the son of Tom Topertoe who becomes a lord upon selling out the Irish Parliament in 1801. Hence, he is a "Union" lord since the honorable men vote against the dissolution of the Dublin Parliament. Lord Cumber lives sumptuously in London while his starving tenants are abused by "Val the Vulture." The O'Regans suffer tragically, being evicted on a stormy Christmas Eve when their seriously ill son Torley is carried out into the snow to die. They find another miserable cabin, but are hounded by M'Clutchy who evicts them again. This eviction scene is even more emotional than the first one because Mary O'Regan is charged by thoughts of her dead son and dying husband. She pleads with Hugh to die quickly and join Torley in Paradise before the yeomen enter the hovel. Hugh dies, but the Orangemen think he is feigning death and attempt to stab his corpse with a bayonet until Mary and Raymond furiously attack the group. In the struggle, the gun goes off and kills a soldier while Mary, crying out in Irish that it is God's strength that is flowing from her body, disarms another soldier and throws him to the floor with her hands tightly fastened around his throat.

"Raymond of the hat," so called because he piles hats upon his head, is like Jemmy in "The Miller of Mohill" (1861), a poor harmless idiot who instinctively sides with the innocent and fights their enemies. He watches the tender scene that follows the departure of the yeomen. Brian, who is also suffering from the fever, trembles after the savage fight and tries to reach his mother, but slips on the bloody floor. Mary removes all traces of the blood, yet the boy is still frightened and asks to be placed near his father to be comforted by his kisses and strong arms. To appease the child, they place him beside Hugh. Brian throws his arms around his father, kissing him until his tears stop. Shortly thereafter, Brian dies. Mary looks on, restrained and detached, and sings in Irish a sweet, melancholy, mournful song. Raymond innocently asks her, "Is the purty boy, the fair-haired boy asleep, or what, tell me."[12] Looking at Raymond, Mary asks him if he is M'Clutchy. He shouts at her that he is. She, as if convulsed, screams horribly and runs at an incredible speed out into the dark night. "It was vain to pursue her; for there was none there capable of doing it with success unless Raymond, who understood not that she had become insane."[13] This powerful scene illustrating the evils of absentee landlordism is unique in the annals of Irish literature.

Lord Cumber in London who expects "money, money, money by any means, but by all means money"[14] rigidly controls his tenants who must vote as instructed; he prefers a Catholic work force because it makes fewer demands for education and civil liberties. He knows that Protestant tenants would be more troublesome because he observes the growing strength of industrial English workers, who are demanding more pay and better working conditions. He is killed in a duel and replaced by his brother Richard who becomes a benevolent resident landlord. Lord Cumber's death atones, in part, for the injustices inflicted upon his honorable workers, a warning to other landlords and agents that they may suffer the same fate unless their governance changes.

When Ned O'Regan returns from England to murder Valentine M'Clutchy, Carleton depicts the act as justifiable homicide, provoked by the needless slaughter of Ned's father and brothers and his mother's death at the grave site of her family. Bonfires are lit to celebrate M'Clutchy's death and the appointment of a just agent by Lord Cumber's brother Richard.

Thirty-one chapters detail the many ways in which the other Catholic families confront the unjust land system and the vain attempts of the Biblemen to convert them. The proselytizing effort is a subplot with a cast of characters headed by Solomon M'Slime, the religious attorney. He eventually defrauds an insurance company of £2000 paid to his family on his alleged death while he emigrates to America with his young maid Susanna. Other noteworthy characters in the religious controversy are Darby O'Drive, the bailiff who is converted to Protestantism, Reverend Phineas Lucre and his curate Mr. Clement, and Reverend Father Roche and his curate Father M'Cabe. The community retains its Catholicism, outwitting the Protestant prelates, who with few exceptions are more interested in collecting the legally proscribed tithes from the Catholic tenants than in instructing them on religious matters.

The fusion of the evils of the tithe system with those of the land system made good propaganda, creating a rallying point for the nationalists. The fictional logic holding the tale together was that charity, the source of social justice, must be practiced by landlord, agent, and tenant before peace could be achieved. The novel does not have a utopian setting peopled by mythical characters without substance. On the contrary, *Valentine M'Clutchy* is set in rural Ireland and demonstrates episodes from the lives of living characters. The raid on the O'Regan cabin is an exaggerated version of Orangemen invading the Carleton cottage; consequently, the novel reinforced Carleton's belief that utopia might be realized in Ireland by the combined efforts of all Irish classes and creeds. The novel with its frequent republications in the nineteenth century presented a comprehensive view of Ireland from the Union of 1801 through the first quarter of the nineteenth century. Carleton's theme, noble as it was, lacked a cast of credible leading characters to work out his ideas, an observation made by a contemporary reviewer in the *Anthenaeum*.[15] The same criticism did not apply to *The Black Prophet*.

The Black Prophet

Carleton returned to a more realistic account of his people in *The Black Prophet* which appeared serially in the *Dublin University Magazine* from May to December, 1846, and was published next year in London, Belfast, and New York as *The Black Prophet, a Tale of Irish Famine*. It has enjoyed a continuing publication with an edition of 1899 introduced by David O'Donaghue and illustrated by Jack Yeats, an Irish translation by Seamus O'Ceallais in 1940, and a facsimile of the 1899 edition with an introduction by Professor Timothy Webb of the University of Leeds in 1972. Since Carleton was not writing here for a religious cause or a national movement, he presented a more natural picture of suffering characters who represent people actually starving on a genocidal scale while Carleton was writing about them. The timely theme features Donnel Dhu (black Daniel), the black prophet who is an elemental figure. His exploits and the episodes from the lives of people undergoing extinction dramatized the theme so forcefully that the novel assumed a classic position in Irish literature despite a weak plot.

Six families interact with each other; five are Catholic: Magennis, M'Ivor-M'Gowan, Murtagh, Dalton, and Sullivan. The Protestant Hendersons are land agents who are more realistic than is Val M'Clutchy. The story begins with a description of the bare hovel in which Donnel, his daughter Sarah, and his wife Nelly, Sarah's stepmother, live. Sarah and Nelly are savagely fighting, and Sarah, almost stabbing Nelly through the heart with an old knife, finally bites her ear to appease her anger. Donnel is not at home during the fight; he is at the Sullivan's cabin foretelling the future of Mave Sullivan, the beautiful nineteen-year-old daughter of Jerry and Bridget Sullivan who have an unnamed number of other children. Donnel represents the class of prophecy men who forecast the future, interpret dreams, analyze political and social events in terms of superstitious beliefs, and look for omens to support their prophecies. He is, however, an evil prophet whose murderous, deceitful, and cunning character promotes his own interests. Unlike Fardorougha, Donnel has a family that reflects his wickedness and complements his treacherous character.

The novel tells a complex tale of hidden identities that builds up suspense and excitement. Donnel Dhu M'Gowan is actually Donnel M'Ivor, separated from his first wife, who comes into the story as the widow Hanlon investigating the death twenty-two years earlier of her brother Peter Magennis. His son, posing as Charley Hanlon, is also investigating the death, following a dream that directs him to M'Gowan's locale. No one knows that Donnel Dhu has murdered Peter Magennis. By coincidence, Bartle Sullivan, Jerry's brother, disappears on the night of the murder, and it is assumed that Condy Dalton killed him although no body is discovered. A generation later, Mave Sullivan and young Condy Dalton fall in love, but Jerry objects to the relationship because he still believes that old Condy killed Bartle. When Nelly digs for dandelions to heal Donnel's face, bruised in a fight with young Condy Dalton, she unearths a skeleton which she believes to be that of Bartle Sullivan. She also thinks Donnel murdered him. For an unexplained reason, except that it is necessary for the denouement, Donnel hides an old tobacco box in the house with the initials "P.M." which connects him with the murder of Peter Magennis.

The Daltons and the Sullivans survive the great hunger, and the ultimate marriage of Mave and Condy following the release of old Condy Dalton from jail (which coincides with the return of Bartle Sullivan) offers some relief to episode after episode of sickness, starvation, and death. One particular chapter, "A Rustic Miser and His Establishment," captures the distress of starving people trying to get grain from Darby Skinadre who looks forward to famine periods so he can sell his grain at inflated prices. Adding insult to injury, Darby informs the people that their failure to attend mass and practice religious rituals causes their misfortune. In this chapter, Carleton describes the Murtaghs' sufferings. Brian and Kathleen Murtagh lose their son Alick, and their only child Peggy is keeping them alive with food begged from charitable neighbors. She loves her parents despite the fact that they refuse to comfort or house her since the illegitimate birth of her daughter, fathered by Condy's brother Tom. Peggy, disowned, dishonored, and dying herself from starvation, asks Skinadre for grain for her parents. He refuses until Tom Dalton, grabbing the miser by the throat and choking him, forces him to give her the meal. Before Peggy can get to her parent's cabin, she collapses and dies. Her daughter dies soon after.

The wake, held at the Murtaghs, brings other poor people together, and they share their food with the couple who have not eaten in two days. They all weep on witnessing the reconciliation of Peggy and her parents who temporarily lose their reason upon seeing her and their grandchild. "Oh! how she loved that child," says Kathleen, "see how she keeps her arm about it, for fear anything might happen to it or that anyone might take it away from her." "I know how she loved it," Brian softly murmurs, "I'll tell you, although I didn't let on to her, still I loved the poor little thing myself—ay, did I."[16] When Tom Dalton suddenly comes into the room, he loudly proclaims that poverty and his father prevented him from marrying Peggy. Brian curses Tom, but Kathleen blesses him because of Peggy's love for him. Soon after, Tom dies and is buried beside Peggy and their infant. The community has few social graces left in its world, disrupted by uncontrollable external forces that break the traditional bonds of love, friendship, and charity; Carleton indicates the extent of the social disintegration in the death scene at the Murtaghs.

The characters in *The Black Prophet* differ markedly from the characters in *Traits and Stories* and *Tales and Sketches* because of the social changes that have taken place. The jolly wakes are replaced by mournful wakes; weddings are discouraged even under Peggy's circumstance; the kitchen gathering described in "The Station" where varieties of food and drink are served is supplanted by the miser's establishment where the starving people are ridiculed for their lack of piety. Carleton's ironic humor in the earlier tales is gone, along with comic dialogue, because the novel is a dirge. The characterization of Mrs. M'Ivor (widow Hanlon), with her need to avenge her brother's death taking precedence over her feelings for her daughter

Sarah, is unique. No other woman in Carleton's fiction denies motherhood as does this woman. The men with their rotting potato crops relieve their frustrations by violent acts triggered by trivial incidents and live on the edge of an abyss engulfing them and their families. The depressed tone of the novel, which is a requiem for a culture, echoes the dying sounds of rural Ireland.

A superficial critique by Webb, who did not comprehend Mave Sullivan's virtue or the discordant combination of vice and virtue in Sarah and Peggy, stated that Donnel Dhu is a Gothic villain.[17] That is not the case. Donnel's characterization is far removed from Gothic villainy, best illustrated in Maturin's work. The Gothic villains, central characters in anti-Catholic novels with traditional props from medieval churches and castles, destroy their victims stylishly. Donnel murders for profit and revenge and is haunted by memories of the event. Donnel, more like Othello, is insanely jealous of his first wife, and this emotional intensity makes him an unfit Gothic villain. His love for Sarah, his failure to satisfactorily abduct Mave Sullivan, and his criminal death further exclude him from the class of Gothic villains. The wretchedness of the Daltons, Sullivans, and Murtaghs occur regardless of Donnel's presence or absence; they are not suffering because of Donnel's villainy. He symbolizes evil in Ireland's blackest period, created from deep within its culture, not from an outmoded literary tradition.

The Black Prophet was written for a purpose. In dedicating it to Lord John Russell, prime minister of Great Britain and Ireland, Carleton states that neglect and illiberal legislation have brought on the calamity which the prime minister has the power to prevent from occurring again. In the preface, the author admits that the novel, published in a time of national destruction of epic proportions, is meant to arouse the reader's sympathy. Carleton, however, adds that famine is not the novel's principle interest, for the main attraction is "the workings of those passions and feelings which usually agitate human life and constitute the character of those who act in it."[18] He was saying that the work is more than a tale of Irish famine to be read like a newspaper article. Showing the politics of Irish famine and the character of passionate people terrorized by death from starvation or emigration were facets of the author's purpose in writing *The Black Prophet*. His next novel spoke to the same issues.

The Emigrants of Ahadarra, a Tale of Irish Life

Carleton vividly told the story of a rural community recovering from the effects of the famine in *The Emigrants of Ahadarra* (1848) by describing the desolation of a town and its attempt at regeneration. The novel is a prose version of Goldsmith's "The Deserted Village." The old problem of land leasing takes on more serious consequences here, because emigration is the only satisfactory option available to farmers who do not secure leases in a nation where "about 800,000 people died from Famine-related causes between 1846 and 1850."[19] The great loss of life did not create a labor shortage because the population had soared from 4 million in 1785 to more than 8 million by the 1840s.[20]

Carleton presents landlord, agent, and tenant free from propagandistic characterizations. The characters more realistically dramatize the evils of the Irish land system than do those in *Valentine M'Clutchy*—the villainy is equally distributed among the various classes and religious sects. The causes of the town's misfortune are not simplified and attributed to wicked Protestant landlords and agents or ignorant Catholic tenants. People have to emigrate. Kiely writes that "there was no remedy but the remedy of flight into an exile where every dream, waking and sleeping, would be poignant with memories of the old places and the abandoned homesteads."[21]

There are six families interacting in this novel of which five are Catholic: Hogan, Peety, Burke, Cavanagh, and M'Mahon; the Clintons are Protestant. Other minor characters—the hedge schoolmaster, still operator, landlords, agents, and parish priests—complete the cast. No single character dominates the tale, which purports to be the story of the M'Mahons' emigration. Philip, Ned, and Bat Hogan with his wife Kate are tinkers who live on Cavanagh's farm. Peety Dhu (Black Peety) and his daughter Nanny are homeless beggars. Jemmy and Rosha Burke are wealthy farmers with two sons, Hycy and Ned. Gerald Cavanagh is a farmer whose daughters Kathleen and

Hannah play important roles. Mr. Clinton is the local gauger who is caring for his orphaned nephew Harry and niece Maria. The gauger, a gray version of Donnel Dhu in *The Black Prophet,* despises the world and acts to promote his own interests. It includes a working relationship with Teddy Phats, a distiller of *poteen* (whiskey). Bridget and Tom M'Mahon, whose family has farmed Ahadarra longer than the landlord has owned the estate, have a son Bryan and daughter Dora who are major characters.

The M'Mahons plan to emigrate following the conspiracy of the Hogan brothers, Hycy Burke, and old Clinton to evict them when they fail to secure leases. The opening scene pictures the anxious M'Mahon family awaiting Tom's return from Dublin where he receives an oral promise from the landlord to renew his lease. After the long walk, Tom is greeted by his affectionate family who invite the neighbors in so that everyone may learn of Dublin. Kiely observes that they talk of the city "as if it was as wonderful to them and as far away as Samarcand or the remote cities of Cathay."[22] The people, so deeply involved in rural matters, are fascinated by Tom's visit to the urban center and expect to hear marvelous stories of the city. At this time, his family, representing the honest and industrious segment of the rural community, is relatively free from worry and care.

Jemmy Burke and his wife Rosha illustrate the intraclass conflict. Mrs. Burke assumes a higher social position than Jemmy whose money allows Rosha to take on attitudes which she transmits to Hycy, the *sportheen.* Ned, their younger son destined for the priesthood, is at school. Hycy is the evil protagonist and, as his mother's pet and father's worry, plays one parent against the other. He has seduced and deserted two women and looks longingly at Kathleen Cavanagh while proposing to Maria Clinton. With an inordinate amount of deceit and cunning, Hycy works with the Hogans and the land agents to bankrupt Byran M'Mahon while assuring him of friendship and help. Nanny who resists Hycy's charm tells her Aunt Kate Hogan and father about Hycy's attempt to seduce her and to ruin Bryan. These three members of the lowest class watch Hycy Burke and collect evidence that ties him to the building of the still at Ahadarra and the robbery of his father's house. Grieving from the shame upon his family, Jemmy gives Hycy a hundred pounds to escape the punishment due his crimes. He emigrates to Canada where he dies in Montreal following a disreputable life. Rosha eventually stops criticizing Jemmy and blaming his vulgar ways for Hycy's downfall. Their son Ned, after leaving the seminary, marries Hannah Cavanagh and operates his father's substantial farm.

Gerald Cavanagh and his wife are social climbers and arrange for Kathleen's marriage to Hycy, telling her she can reform him, but realizing they are sacrificing their daughter to a dishonorable man. The parents, resigned to Kathleen's refusal to consider Hycy, then plan for her marriage to Ned Burke in order to raise their station in life despite Kathleen's love for Bryan M'Mahon. Mrs. Cavanagh rationalizes Hycy's behavior by saying the ruined women caused their own fate and Kathleen is imagining insults where none were intended by Hycy. Kathleen and Hannah, shocked by their mother's acceptance of Hycy's immorality, console each other in trying to understand her remarks. Without the parental matchmaking, Ned Burke marries Hannah, which, of course, is just as pleasing to the Cavanaghs. Kathleen, however, holds up her marriage to Bryan when she believes he is attacking his religion and country by voting for a Tory candidate who had helped him with the law when an illegal still was discovered on his farm. She refuses to listen to his defense against the slander that Hycy and the Hogans circulate about him. Her rigid and irrational Catholicism destroys their chance of happiness. Her excessive piety and confusion about religion and economics document the unresolvable conflicts that complicate the lives of religious and patriotic women. Because of Kathleen, her brother James is unable to express his love for Bryan's sister Dora, and the two moral families are at a standstill. The Cavanaghs and M'Mahons resemble the O'Donovans and O'Briens in *The Black Prophet* in that the intraclass conflicts within the Catholic culture generate much of the unhappiness of the trapped characters.

The M'Mahon family has the dominant role in the novel. Bryan is intelligent and industrious, resembling Connor O'Donovan in *Fardorougha the Miser*. Bryan is also a naive character who does not recognize Hycy's evil intentions or the agent's duplicity in denying the land lease. When the legal problems arise, Bryan allows Hycy to handle the appeal with the magistrates. Harry Clinton, the gauger's nephew and Hycy's friend, recognizes his treacherous nature and breaks the relationship, forcing his uncle to vindicate Bryan and acknowledge Hycy's guilt.

The death of Bridget M'Mahon, who blesses each of her children and Kathleen Cavanagh and tries to prepare her husband Tom to live without her, is a great scene. He is inconsolable and attempts to postpone her burial until his aged father forcibly tells him to act like a man and bear his grief. Tom is never the same man again. On the eve of his expected departure to America, Tom walks to Bridget's grave and tells her his body will be buried in a strange land, but their eternal souls will be together. Crying in Irish to his dead wife, the unhappy husband says he is leaving so their children may live in a free and prosperous country. Grandfather M'Mahon is the last to learn of the emigration, and he experiences a sudden flash of reason called the "lightening before death" which predicts the family's destiny. Before anyone can move old Bryan, the patriarch dies. His wake delays the emigration while his predictions are being implemented.

Several long authorial intrusions convey Carleton's ideas about the causes of emigration and the practice of subletting, which allows a small farmer to divide his holdings equally with his children. Within two generations, more families are farming on holdings too small to maintain a decent standard of living, and a severe socioeconomic situation worsens. Generalizing, Carleton says that landlords permit subdividing to produce more votes. Like "Frankenstein in the novel it pursues them to the present moment, and must be satisfied or appeased in some way, or it will unquestionably destroy them." (*W*, 2:572).

Carleton is remembering the desolation of Clogher Valley, seen when he visited his family and friends in 1846. Although O'Finigan, the schoolmaster, breaks the seriousness of the novel, most of the characters are determined, frustrated, unhappy beings caught in the social whirlpool. The deaths, wakes, and funerals of Bridget and old Bryan M'Mahon are high dramatic episodes in the novel, along with the thrashing given to Bryan by the Catholic congregation because he dares to vote for his economic interest. The landlords of these people, according to Carleton, hold the key to their prosperity. They must forbid future subdivisions and realize their "duty to prevent Irish interests from being made subservient to English interests, and from being legislated for upon English principles." (*W,* 2:630).

In writing this novel specifically for the Simms and McIntyre publishing firm in Belfast, Carleton was courting a northern Irish audience which could more readily identify with the agrarian unrest than a Dublin audience. O'Donoghue, Carleton's biographer, rated it as one of his best novels because of the fine character studies, moving scenes, and freedom "from the bad taste, coarseness and rancour which occasionally blemish his works" (*L,* 2:101). Digby Starkey, Carleton's friend, found a tone of good feeling throughout the novel, enabling landlord, tenant, and agent to cordially work out their problems. Although puzzled by Hycy's character, he thought Kathleen, O'Finigan, plain honest Jemmy, and Kate Hogan were remarkable characters and that the death of the Irish patriarch displayed a "close study of Irish character; the humour, too, all throughout, is eminently happy" (*L,* 2:102). In other words, these characters represent a rational approach to the agrarian problems to be solved by all classes.

Chapter Five
The Later Novels

*The Tithe Proctor, a Novel, Being a Tale
of the Tithe Rebellion in Ireland*

The nationalist fervor of *Valentine M'Clutchy* and the neutral
tone of *The Emigrants of Ahadarra* were soon replaced by the
vituperative quality of *The Tithe Proctor* (1849) which attacked
Catholic farmers and servants in the Whiteboy Society. Contra-
dicting his former support of the national movement, Carleton
was responding to his financial needs. Hopelessly in debt, he
petitioned the British government for a pension based on his
literary accomplishment. To his credit, the memorial was signed
by the nationalists, conservatives, the Catholic archbishop of
Dublin, Catholic bishop of Clogher, high-ranking Anglican
clergy, the provost of Trinity College, the president of Maynooth, the lord mayor of Dublin, the attorney-general, and
eighty-year-old Maria Edgeworth. Accepting an English pension put Carleton under obligations that restricted future
literary growth. After obtaining the £200 a year award on June
23, 1848, *The Tithe Proctor,* a venomous product, was published. Had the novel appeared before the memorial, signatures
of the Catholic clergy and John O'Connell, Daniel's son, would
hardly have been affixed.

Religion had long been a divisive factor in Irish society, and
the laws that forced the Catholic population to pay 10 percent
of its earnings to the Anglican clergy contributed much to the
hostile relationships. Men hired to collect the tithes from the
unwilling Catholics were called tithe proctors, and it was not
unusual to find Catholics in this position because of the steady
income earned from the unpleasant task. This novel tells, from
a bizarre viewpoint, the story of a Catholic tithe proctor and his
family. Never being sure of the author's intention, one wonders
about the relevance of the unconnected series of murderous

acts and violent deeds that are dramatized from Irish history. In the preface, Carleton says that the episodes should not give any serious offense to anyone but expects that some one will find something objectionable. He considers it his public duty to disclose the massacres of the Tithe Rebellion of 1832, the murder of Michael Boland, a Catholic tithe proctor, in 1808, and the Repeal Movement of 1842, all in this novel.

Carleton denounces the pseudopatriots' dedication to the repeal of the Union and blames their agitation for the loss of Irish morality. He says, "The Irishmen of the present day—the creature of agitation is neither honest, nor candid, nor manly, nor generous, but a poor skulking dupe, at once slavish and insolent, offensive and cowardly—who carries, as a necessary consequence, the principles of political dishonesty into the practices of private life and is consequently disingenuous and fraudulent" (*W*, 2:362). He fails to describe the villainous English and Irish Protestants who legislated the incredible tax on a people already suffering from barbarous civil and political legislation.[1] Reverend Jeremiah Turbot who is characterized as an absentee Anglican priest living luxuriously in Dublin on the collected tithes does not play a major role in the novel, but he and the Westminster politicians should have been portrayed if one is to take seriously Carleton's statement about his love of truth. As the novel reads, however, all the villains are Catholics motivated by greed, lust, vengeance, and hatred. Frank M'Carthy, a Trinity College law student, is a passive individual wandering in and out of the story.

There are only two Catholic families involved: Mat Purcel, his wife Nancy, and their children John, Alick, Mary, and Julia; and Magistrate Fitzgerald O'Driscol and his children Fergus and Catherine. The opening scene introduces Buck English, a mysterious, unemployed, homeless man who has money and boasts of his friendship with Counsellor O'Connell who advises the people to hold back their tithes to starve out the established church. Buck English's activities are based upon the exploits of a historical figure from Limerick with the same name, famous for his leadership of the rebel forces in the 1798 Revolution.

On this particular Sunday morning in Carleton's novel, Buck, in high English, addresses Mrs. Purcel and her daughters, assisting them from their carriage as they walk into the Catholic chapel. Mat Purcel, a nominal Catholic, sees no difference between Catholicism and Anglicanism and defends Frank M'Carthy's conversion to Protestantism which allows him to enter Trinity College from which Catholics are excluded. The tithe proctor assures his wife that religion must not stand in the way of their children's advancement, and the conversation about religion concludes with Julia reminding her father of the difference between the Catholic priests and the Anglican clergy who hire Purcel. Carleton initially presents a sympathetic picture of the Purcel family. Industrious Mat becomes a tithe proctor to increase his land holdings and to establish his children. His sons are model Irishmen, unrivaled in "symmetry of figure, strength, courage, manly beauty, and gentlemanly bearing" (W, 2:372). Their strength controls the country people, who are horsewhipped if necessary to collect the tithes. The beautiful daughters are well educated and assist their mother in charitably caring for the sick and the poor in the parish.

Magistrate Fitzgerald O'Driscol, comically presented as a cowardly judge whose position is due to past services to the Protestant ascendancy, writes fictional accounts of his accomplishments for the local paper. Fergus tells his father that the stereotyped paragraphs do not ingratiate him with the government. To which the magistrate replies, "In spite of your staryrayotypes, it is such articles . . . that constitute the force of public opinion" (W, 2:418). Fergus agrees that public opinion influences government, but does not believe the articles flattering his father are public opinions. O'Driscol insists that they are and informs Fergus that he knows how to play the game and expects to get a government position for him. Working for the Dublin government means that Fitzgerald O'Driscol alerts it to conspiracies in his district while maintaining a sense of fairness with the laboring class. One scene dramatizes the magistrate's dilemma, forcing him to decide between John Purcel and Darby Hourigan who has been horsewhipped by Purcel. Searching for information about a conspiracy from Purcel and quaking from a threatening letter from Darby's friends, he lets Purcel off with a fine which is acceptable to both parties.

Darby Hourigan, Frank Finnerty, Mark Ratigan (alias Phil

Hart), Mogue Moylan, and Billy Bradly are members of the Whiteboy force headed by Buck English (Captain Right) that attacks Purcel's house. They challenge an evil judicial system that denies civil and political liberties and enforces tithing. One gruesome scene in which Billy Bradly retells his role in the murder of Callaghan, another Catholic tithe proctor, is dramatically presented. The legs of a half dozen tomcats are drawn down, up, and across Callaghan's naked back and sides, and then his bleeding body is thrown in a grave lined with thorns. He is buried alive. Not all of the Whiteboys listening to the story accept the cruelties, but they continue their membership in the society because there is no other option. In the novel, Carleton also records the murder of Murray, a Catholic farmer who pays the tithe, by the Whiteboys who have selected a young boy to commit the crime. He is captured and executed, and his mother dies of a broken heart.

The characters who foil the Whiteboys are Jerry Joyce, a Whiteboy and Purcel's servant, and the Cannie Soogah (jolly peddler), twin brother to Buck English, and leader of another group of Whiteboys. The Cannie Soogah is an interesting character who heads the nonviolent resistance to the tithe system and tries to save M'Carthy and the Purcels. He shoots Hourigan and Ratigan, O'Driscol's servants, to save M'Carthy's life and amasses a thousand Whiteboys to prevent the raid on the Purcels. The assault, however, occurs and is graphically described. Mat and John Purcel are slain by a volley of bullets, and Buck English is killed during the attack. Jerry Joyce kills Moylan who is running away with Julia Purcel, and Alick Purcel escapes death by blackening his face and donning a white shirt to blend in with the Whiteboys. The Cannie Soogah arrives too late to prevent the murders, but he assumes control of the situation. Mrs. Purcel, Alick, Mary, Julia, and M'Carthy are taken to O'Driscol's home. His terror on seeing so many Whiteboys approaching his house drives him to the darkest corner of the coal hole in the cellar, and he stays there until a search party finds him.

At the conclusion of the novel, Carleton unites Alick Purcel and Catherine O'Driscol in matrimony, and at a later date when he finishes his studies, M'Carthy marries Julia Purcel. There is no resolution, though, of the social conflicts. It is difficult to combine the disparate segments and to imagine a satisfactory ending. Certainly the characterization of M'Carthy is incredibly stupid; he is unable to recognize danger or take an active role in defending the Purcels. His adventures with the Whiteboys add suspense to the story, but his imprudent bravado would merit instant death without the Cannie Soogah's protection. M'Carthy's character contains elements of Carleton's character in that the Trinity College student does not allow religion to block his career and associates with people who are on good terms with the government. The priests and parsons in the tale are on much better terms than the proctor and his victims, as the scene describing Father Anthony's midnight call to Mr. Goodison's starving family indicates.

There are many villains in the story—the servants, the proctor and his sons, the Whiteboys who are anachronistic O'Connellites—but no heroes. It is false, of course, to associate O'Connell with violence because he preached nonviolence throughout his long career, seeking legal means to redress injustices.[2] The Cannie Soogah, a generous moral man, spends most of his time in the novel as an itinerant peddler, one who likes to please the women and kiss the servants. He does not have heroic characteristics, and yet he functions as the moral force in the community. Except for the weak social relationship between the Purcels and the O'Driscols, there is no society to speak of in *The Tithe Proctor*. Although the deaths of Mat and John Purcel, Buck English, and Mogue Moylan are relevant to the novel, the torture and death of Callaghan and the massacre at Carrickshock are isolated scenes irrelevant to the literary nature of the novel. Carleton's schizophrenic attitude toward his culture is illustrated best in this confused tale.

The critical response to *The Tithe Proctor* was not favorable. O'Donoghue thought it exhibits the "worse passions of the people, a rancorous description of the just war" (*L*, 2:120), doing more harm to Carleton's reputation than any other work. His biographer actually suggested that Carleton may have been suffering a mental aberration while writing this perverted version of the antitithe period, but a contemporary saw the novel differently. The reviewer in the *Athenaeum* (April 21, 1849) suspected that the novel signified that a political truce had been reached and predicted that no more novels condemning the government's mismanagement of Ireland were going to be written. Father Stephen J. Brown, an Irish bibliographer, assumed that the novel was composed "in a mood of savage resentment against his countrymen."[3] Flanagan found the tone raging and sulphurous at times with Purcel's portrait etched in acid, but he said, "Carleton's anger is directed against rebels and landlords alike."[4] Boué said, "Du point de vue artistique, *The Tithe Proctor* est imparfait" (From an artistic point of view, *The Tithe Proctor* is imperfect).[5] An insightful criticism from William Bradley, however, related the similarity of Purcel's world to contemporary North Ireland where injustices again trigger secret societies. Bradley thought the novel worth reading because "it at least demonstrates the nature and magnitude of the problems confronting a divided society like ours."[6] From this perspective, a reader may find it worthwhile to read *The Tithe Proctor,* but the novel lacks the quality of the earlier works. In his next novel, Carleton assumed an entirely different attitude as he related the story of an Irish hero.

Willy Reilly and His Dear Colleen Bawn, a Tale Founded upon Fact

The romantic story of Willy Reilly and his beloved, written shortly after the scathing novel of the tithe rebellion of the 1830s, is the theme of *Willy Reilly* (1850, 1855). It is a fine novel marked with characteristics of Carleton's best work: a moving narrative, a temperate tone, excellent descriptive passages, credible characters, and a judicious use of dialogue to tell the story. Carleton's strength here overpowers his weaknesses: the altering of geographic localities, explanatory digressions to explain his feelings or present historical data, and the excessive use of coincidental events. "Willy Reilly and his Dear Cooleen [*sic*] Bawn" (Fair-Haired Girl) first appeared in a London magazine, the *Independent* (December 1850 and January 1851). The tale expands upon the ballad of "Willy Reilly and the Colleen Bawn."[7] The first version in the *Independent* is sketchy. Carleton added to it for the first edition of the novel published in 1855 and later included the subplot, which records the romance of Fergus Reilly and Ellen Connor, in the second edition of 1857.

In the preface to the first edition, Carleton reprints fifteen stanzas of the ballad and tells of its enduring popularity among the rural population. He hopes the story does not express any political sentiment that may offend any party, "an attempt of singular difficulty in a country so miserably divided upon religious feeling" (*W*, 1:2). He also informs the reader that, upon learning that priests may never be disguised as women even to save their lives, he changes with one exception those scenes in which priests are disguised as women in order to elude the priest hunters. In the preface to the second edition, Carleton gratefully acknowledges *Willy Reilly*'s favorable reception by the public and the critics, citing his debt to Dr. John O'Donovan for the historical data about the O'Reilly family. Furthermore, since the tale is considered a historical novel although not intended as such, Carleton offers information about the penal laws of the period which prohibit and void all intermarriages between Catholics and Protestants. The laws were "spurned not only by human reason, but by human passion" (*W*, 1:5).

The novel opens with two travelers slowly making their way through an impenetrable fog. They are later identified as Squire Alexander Folliard and his faithful servant Andy Cummisky. The squire is the father of Helen, the colleen bawn (spelled throughout the novel, on the title page, and in the ballad as *cooleen*). He is one of the anti-Catholic landlords who, hating popery, nevertheless hires mostly Catholics to manage his estate and operate his household. At times, he hides priests from their pursuers, yet as a magistrate, he has exiled a priest for performing an intermarriage ceremony. The squire has a mercurial temperament and is easily angered or persuaded to change his opinion by more aggressive characters. He is neither a villain nor a hero, and his love for Helen is the dominant passion in his widowhood, conflicting with his hatred for Catholics.

The Folliard family, representing the Protestant landed gentry, is the dominant family. It interacts with Sir Robert Whitecraft, a genuine villain, who is another Protestant landowner living three miles from the Folliards. He is about forty years old and leaves London to press his courtship of beautiful Helen who is not yet twenty years old. While in Ireland, he enforces the penal laws and represents the English politicians of the eighteenth century who have enacted the crippling legislation. William Reilly, a Catholic landowner, is the only member of his illustrious family characterized in the novel, and he is the hero of the tale, being a strong intelligent man who falls in love with Helen. The Folliards, Whitecraft, and Reilly are the major characters. The Browns and Hastings, benevolent Protestant families, play minor roles in counteracting the evil deeds of Whitecraft and Mr. Smellpriest who relentlessly search for the Catholic clergy. The minor Catholic characters are the Red Rapparee, or Randy O'Donnel, Fergus Reilly, Widow Buckley, Ellen Connor, Lanigan, Andy Cummiskey, and Tom Steeple.

Sir Robert Whitecraft visits the Folliards to subtly work on the squire's prejudices in order to discredit Willy. Knowing that Folliard hates Jesuits, Whitecraft tells him that Reilly is a Jesuit having been educated on the Continent by them; he also says that Reilly has planned an assault upon the squire. Folliard turns against Reilly and is going to execute him for such a bold plan. Helen gets Tom Steeple, the village fool whose only ambition is to be tall, hence the name, to warn Reilly. He is also warned by Fergus Reilly, a former member of O'Donnel's band. Willy Reilly must flee from Ireland and makes a clandestine visit to Helen who wants to join him. He rejects the idea as being foolhardy and tells her to stay with her father until the penal laws are changed, recognizing he is powerless against White-craft and O'Donnel who have already searched his home for papers to transfer the estate. Unable to find any, they burn the house and double their effort to find Reilly who is hiding with the widow Buckley; he is eventually captured and jailed.

Meanwhile, the squire goes on with the plans to marry Helen to Sir Robert. The marriage does not occur because Sir Robert Whitecraft, arrested for his many crimes, is lodged in the same jail with Reilly. At the jury trial, because Sir Robert is hated by Protestants, the Protestant jury condemns him to death. The squire immediately plans an appeal to Dublin and demands that Reilly be executed. One fine scene pictures Helen in court where she testifies against her father; her testimony changes Willy's sentence from death to seven years' exile. After the court appearance, Helen loses her sanity which finally alters her father's opinion of Reilly.

Helen's mind is fixed on finding Reilly. Whenever she meets a man, she asks if he can tell her where William Reilly is. The best doctors cannot cure her irrationality, and her grieving father blames himself for her condition. He resembles Bodagh O'Brien in *Fardorougha the Miser* whose refusal to sanction his daughter Una's marriage to Connor O'Donovan almost causes her death. Time passes, and in seven-and-a-half years Willy Reilly returns to Ireland, restores himself to his estate with Hastings' cooperation, and looks for his colleen bawn. At their dramatic meeting, only a few minutes pass before Helen, who asks her usual question, is convinced she has found her lover. With her father's approval, she is married by Reverend Brown and a Catholic priest to Willy Reilly. Ellen Connor and Fergus Reilly also marry and live with the couple. At Folliard's death three years later, the two Reilly couples emigrate to the Continent, where Willy and Helen have a large family of sons who serve admirably in European armies. Thus ends the tale of Willy Reilly and his fair-haired girl.

Willy Reilly, totally different from Carleton's novels of the cabin culture, is a historical novel in the tradition of Griffin's *The Invasion* (1832) set in the eighth century and *The Duke of Mommouth* (1836) set in 1685, and the Banims' *The Boyne Water* (1826) set at the end of the seventeenth century during the Williamite Wars, *The Croppy* (1828) set during the penal age of the eighteenth century, and *The Denounced* (1830) which covers the period during the Rebellion of 1798. Carleton may also be compared with the Dubliner Joseph Sheridan Le Fanu whose *The Cock and Anchor, a Chronicle of Old Dublin* (1850) portrays the immorality and political corruption rampant in Swift's eighteenth-century Dublin, the nerve center of convulsing Ireland. *Willy Reilly* was a rural counterpart of *The Cock and Anchor.* Carleton carefully selected a theme that could not insult any living Irishman. Since the penal age was a result of the actions of former English politicians, *Willy Reilly* was not apt to insult contemporary politicians who had passed the Catholic Emancipation Act in 1829. There are enough moral Protestants in the novel to offset immoral Sir Robert Whitecraft, and Willy Reilly, a Catholic gentleman of heroic proportions, compensates for the treachery of Randy O'Donnel; consequently, neither Protestants nor Catholics complained about attacks upon their religion. The theme was a happy one, too, in that it related past injustices that no longer existed, leading the reader to believe that the difficulties of the 1850s would also pass. Carleton's historical novel was different from earlier novels in another dimension, the dialogue. He did not use Irish idiom or phrases so common in the tales of contemporary life. Most of the eighteenth-century rural people were speaking Irish, but Carleton could not use that language in writing for an English reading public; so, he used the English language with only a trace of the Irish dialect or none at all. Lanigan, the squire's cook, for instance, speaks English. On telling Helen to quiet her emotions as she prepares to flee with Reilly, Lanigan says, "Well, Miss Folliard: but for God's sake, don't cry so; your eyes will get red, and your father may notice it" (*W*, 1:128). The Scottish gardener who surpervises Reilly is the only character speaking in dialect: "Come wi' me and Masther Lanigan here, and we'll see what you ken about the sceentific profession" (*W*, 1:105). One expecting the blistering hyperbolic speech of Carleton's contemporary characters is sure to be disappointed with the country characters in *Willy Reilly;* but since the novel does not purport to be a realistic tale about people and events known to the author, the disappointment need not be great.

Remarks, though, link eighteenth-century Sligo with nineteenth-century Tyrone. Andy Morrow from "Ned M'Keown" appears in the novel when a renter says, "I took this cottage, and the bit of land that goes with it, from honest Andy Morrow" (*W*, 1:148). And in directing Smellpriest to a cottage where a priest is hiding, Reverend Samson Strong, who sends the militia captain out so he can make love to Mrs. Smellpriest, tells him to go to Houlaghan's strip of land in Kilrudden, the site of Ned M'Keown's house.

Willy Reilly had a long publishing history, including American editions in 1855, 1856, 1875, 1880, 1881, 1884, and 1970 from which Carleton and his heirs received not a shilling. Despite frequent reprintings of the novel in London and Dublin and the pirated reprinting in the *Limerick Examiner* of the first version in the London magazine, Carleton was inadequately compensated. The popular novel evoked a mixed critical response. O'Donaghue stated "It is not at all a first-rate novel" (*L*, 2:199), for other than Reilly, he felt, there was hardly another good character. Yet Helen Folliard stands out as a strong character, emotionally torn between Reilly and her father. She has the intelligence to understand her father's weakness and Whitecraft's control over him and the character to testify for Willy. Ellen Connor, Fergus Reilly, and Andy Cummiskey are credible minor characters whose loyalty to their masters is exemplary. The dying Captain Smellpriest, who spits blood into the face of Reverend Strong, letting him know he is aware of his wife's infidelity, is a memorable character.

A contemporary reviewer in the *Athenaeum* (May 5, 1855) noted that the novel is good, illustrating Irish chivalry at its best through noble Willy's romantic characterization. However, André Boué believed that the novel is mediocre and repeated most of O'Donoghue's sentiments while saying that the tone is a pleasant contrast to most of his novels, "Mais le ton mesuré l'absence presque totale de polémique, tranchent agréablement avec l'amertume et l'agressivité de la plupart de ses romans" (But the measured tone and the almost total absence of polemic contrasts nicely with the bitterness and aggression in most of his novels).[8] It is very difficult to evaluate as mediocre a novel that has a genuine hero whose integrity is admired by servants, the sheriff, the jailer, and, of course, his colleen bawn. Carleton, keeping in mind the heroic exploits of Willy Reilly known throughout Connaught and Ulster, created a work that does justice to the hero and the theme.

Willy interacts with the Folliards, the Protestant gentry, servants, the persecuted priests, and the Red Rapparee. Prudently, he avoids Sir Robert Whitecraft, unlike Frank M'Carthy in *The Tithe Proctor* who rashly challenges his adversaries. Self-reliant Reilly depends upon his moral and physical strength (he has beaten the Red Rapparee in a fight) to sustain himself and protect his friends. He knows, too, that at times discretion is the better part of valor and withdraws when, in his judgment, he cannot accomplish his objective. No other heroic character from the four great novels—Connor Donovan, Richard Topertoe, Condy Dalton, and Bryan M'Mahon—is as well developed and involved in so many adventures to demonstrate a unique set of qualities. Carleton's intricate plot in *Willy Reilly,* marred though it is by coincidences (which is true of most of his plots), reveals his protagonist's character. Amply tested, Carleton's

Willy Reilly retains the chivalric character of the historical figure popularized in the ballad, and this is enhanced by the disciplined tone of the novel. The book's fame rests upon its rational approach to an irrational period of Irish history in which a famous hero overcomes the combined evil forces of the aristocracy and the populace.

The Squanders of Castle Squander

Two installments of *The Squanders of Castle Squander* appeared in the *Illustrated London News* (January 1852), but they were not continued. Dr. Robert Shelton MacKenzie, a London friend of Carleton, found this frustrating and damaging to his literary reputation; "The beauty of a 'to-be-continued' story," MacKenzie noted in a letter to Carleton, "consists in the regularity of its appearance."[9] Later in the year, the entire story was published in two volumes for the Illustrated London Library edition, but the novel was poorly received. It had a short publication history and falls outside the category of Carleton's memorable fiction, although some excellent scenes and witty dialogue are scattered throughout the novel. The most serious shortcomings are the dearth of credible characterizations among the gentry or the tenantry and the inferior handling of a theme that Maria Edgeworth manipulated perfectly in *Castle Rackrent*. The old characters—hedge school-masters, land agents, hypocritical religious attorneys, and converts who find Protestantism a means to financial security—are misplaced in this work which focuses upon the imprudent Squanders and their inability to maintain their estate. Because of the superabundant digressions on the problems of land ownership which include statistics and excerpts from social commentaries, the novel loses its literary quality and becomes a platform for Carleton's diatribe against Ireland.

Harry Squander, his wife, their lecherous sons who impregnate four Irish servants while promising rent relief to their families, and their spendthrift daughter Emily who charms Dr. McClaret, making him wish he were a bishop so he can shower her with gifts, are the insolvent residents of Castle Squander. Old Squire Squander, who marries the daughter of Lord Mount Gallivant, a notorious debaucher, initiates the fall of the House of Squander. His wife, although an aristocrat, has no fortune, spends most of her husband's money, and develops Harry's taste for luxuries beyond his income. On inheriting the estate, Harry ignores the advice of his Uncle Tom Squander who tells him to treat his tenants kindly. If the tenants, the source of his wealth, are cared for, they will be loyal, work properly, and be an asset, according to Tom Squander, but Harry sees them as killers poised behind a hedge ready to slay him when an opportune circumstance arrives. Harry Squander and his family know that their needs are greater than their tenants' and believe that tenants exist to accommodate their masters' needs. Thus, the Squanders look upon their tenants as farmers view their workhorses.

Randy O'Rollick, the bailiff's son, makes some value judgments about religion which indicates that Carleton was swinging back to his polemics about Catholics and Protestants. In this instance, Randy favors the Irish Presbyterians because their religious principles are based on reason, whereas Catholics demonstrate an unrestrained emotional piety. These religious feelings, Randy observes, carry over into their social and business life, which means that Presbyterians are industrious and thoughtful, whereas Catholics are irrational. Carleton in *The Squanders of Castle Squander* has a good word for the ardent Orangeman Bob Clendinning who, while hating Catholics and trying to force them out of Ireland, nevertheless does not cheat a papist because it is against his conscience. The author also depicts the Irish beggars who, not too far removed from the Dublin slum dwellers, are classless drifters without a sense of place or destiny.

Bill-in-the Bowl, the legless beggar king, symbolizes the paralyzed nation, unable to move out of the depression that follows bad land management. Billy tells his group that he has as much right to be prime minister in the new Ireland as anyone. He rejects the young revolutionaries who are agitating for change, because once in office they will do nothing for the poor other than tell them to assert their patriotic feelings. Carleton condemns the revolutionary movement, but it is not done without a trace of humor when he is discussing O'Connell's relationship to the Young Irelanders: "'Why don't you put down these young Irelanders?' said a friend of his one day on his return home from a meeting of the Repeal Association. 'What!' he replied, 'Would you have me commit infanticide?' "[10] Randy O'Rollick, Bob Clendinning, and Bill-in-the Bowl are characterizations of lower-class men who are living in the Squanders' world and imitating their behavior. This perplexing plot in which the dregs of Irish society cavort has a bitter ending, enforcing Carleton's damnation of Irish society while praising the "munificent generosity of England and of her princely merchants"[11] during the three years of famine.

There is no argument about Kiely's conclusion that *The Squanders of Castle Squander* is "among the worst of Carleton's later, inferior works."[12] He saw it as a treatise on the Irish land system dramatizing the persons responsible for the problems rather than a novel written to create literary characters. To Boué, the novel was evidence that the better writing days were over: "Le genie de Carleton y apparait sur son decline" (Carleton's genius appears here on the decline).[13] O'Donoghue believed the work makes painful reading although some passages reminded him of the earlier great novels. "Carleton returns to the bad old habit," his biographer says, "of trying to convert readers to his political and religious views by vituperation and invective" (*L,* 2:178). He observes that the novel superficially resembles Lever's work, but Carleton's novel lacks Lever's good-humored approach to the subject and is filled with savage hate and bitterness. The overall evaluation was unanimous: *The Squaders of Castle Squander* is a poor novel, neither offering any fresh insight into the problems of the land lease system nor giving new forms to worn ideas.

Incredibly, Carleton in the latter part of the novel does not even attempt to fictionalize his feelings. He attacks people whose beliefs he opposes. The novel indicates much about Carleton's personality: raging, insecure, isolated, groping, demanding, vengeful, and offensive. These traits made enemies of friends and alienated him from the public, looking for entertainment from its artists and position papers from its politicians. These undesirable characteristics, however, did not represent his total personality; Carleton could also be kind, sociable, generous, and unassuming when his financial burdens were light and the public expressed its appreciation of his works. The novel lacks originality, forcible ideas, and a semblance of

credible characterization. Carleton tried to grasp the totality of
the Irish culture and to synthesize thought with environment,
illuminated by people and places, but because the vituperative
critical aspect of his personality directed the synthesis, no
cultural totality was depicted. Edgeworth, Lady Morgan, Lever,
and Lover are so much better in re-creating what the upper class
thought about itself and the physical world. Two cousins, Edith
Somerville and Violet Martin, under the literary name of
Somerville and Ross, later in the century effectively dramatized
the lives of the Protestant gentry. Their *The Real Charlotte*
(1889), depicting Charlotte's villainy and her disastrous effect
upon tenants and friends, was much more realistic. Against this
standard of excellence, Carleton's portrait of the evil Protestant
landowners in *The Squanders of Castle Squander* was decidedly
inferior.

Red Hall or The Baronet's Daughter, Revised as *The Black Baronet or The Chronicles of Ballytrain*

This novel had a complicated publication history beginning in
1848 when Carleton agreed to write for £210 a novel that
James McGlashan, a Scottish bookseller in Dublin who was
Lever's publisher, requested of him. He started the novel in
1849 and entitled it *The Black Baronet or Chronicles of Ballytrain,*
presenting several chapters that McGlashan printed but did not
like. Consequently, he asked Carleton to make revisions in the
tale which, according to the author, would weaken the story.
They were not done. Since Carleton had given McGlashan the
copyright of an unwritten novel, which he refused to print and
Carleton refused to alter, an impasse was reached. Carleton,
unable to get it published in Dublin, took *The Black Baronet*
with him to London in 1850 along with *Willy Reilly* and *The
Squanders* and sold all three of them to English publishers.

Saunders and Otley published *The Black Baronet* as *Red Hall*
(1852), but their Irish agent held a seven-year copyright on the
novel. An attorney for the London firm advised Carleton of a
threatened law suit and also expressed the firm's anger about a
simultaneous cheap printing of another new Carleton work for
five shillings, *The Squanders,* by another London publisher. It
was competing with the deluxe edition of *Red Hall* offered at a

guinea. In each instance, Carleton acted out of ignorance rather than deceit. Later, the firm refused to reissue the novel in a popular edition, and in 1855, James Blackwood, a London publisher of cheap series of out-of-print books, offered to reprint it for a small fee. Carleton refused the offer. Eventually, James Duffy published it in 1857 under its original title, *The Black Baronet or Chronicles of Ballytrain,* following McGlashan's death in 1856. Duffy reprinted the novel in 1858 and 1875, and American publishers reissued it in 1858, 1880, 1881, and as part of *William Carleton's Works,* in 1970.

With Duffy's editing, *Red Hall* underwent a revision to update it and change the title since Sir Thomas Gourlay is unquestionably the major character and evil protagonist of the tale, the longest and most intricate of Carleton's novels. Carleton tells the reader in the preface that the work exhibits the "three most powerful passions that can agitate the human heart—love, ambition and revenge" (*W,* 1:320).

Three families act upon one another—the plebian Catholic Corbets, the aristocratic Protestant Gourlays, and the Earl of Gullamore, his nephew, and his son Lord Dunroe—in a tangled series of events that are incomprehensible until the denouement in the last chapter. The frequent disguises, name changes, and deceit in normal social relationships that are part of *Willy Reilly* become a major characteristic of *The Black Baronet,* making it a mystery tale rather than a novel of manners or historical novel. The action, set in rural Ireland of 1850, occurs at Red Hall, Sir Thomas's estate; Glenshee Castle, the Earl of Cullamore's estate four miles distant; Anthony Corbet's Dublin shop; the inn at Ballytrain; Sam Robert's Wicklow cottage; the London lodging of Lord Dunroe; and undescribed places in France.

Thomas Gourlay assumes the estate after his brother Edward's death and the disappearance of his son Edward. About the same time, Thomas Gourlay's son Tom is kidnapped, leaving him with one child, the beautiful and virtuous Lucy. The Earl of Cullamore, a just man, has two children, the immoral Lord Dunroe and moral Lady Emily who loves Ensign Roberts, son of a retired military man and his wife living in Wicklow. Lord Dunroe is engaged to Lucy Gourlay.

Lady Gourlay, Edward's widow, learns that her son is alive

and Sir Thomas knows it. Young Edward has escaped from the Dublin madhouse where Gourlay had placed him. Anthony Corbet, a Dublin shopkeeper and former servant to Sir Thomas's father, is involved in Edward's incarceration. He is the most diabolical of the villainous Corbets and executes a complex plot to avenge Sir Thomas's seduction of his daughter Jacinta and his refusal to supply money to bury his illegitimate son born to Jacinta.

Sir Thomas threatens to kill himself if Lucy rejects Dunroe, and Lucy, torn between her love for another man and her father, chooses to obey him. Lord Dunroe does not love Lucy but will marry her for her estate. Shortly before the marriage, the Corbets pass off Ambrose Gray, really his illegitimate son whose death has been fabricated, to Sir Thomas as his lost son. Since Gray looks and acts like the baronet, the deception succeeds. The baronet changes the marriage contract to state that his son will inherit the estate.

Meanwhile, Lord Dunroe discovers he will not inherit Glencree Castle because of his illegitimate birth. Consequently, the marriage in which Lucy is to sacrifice herself is a double fraud. She will not be a countess, and Lord Dunroe is not Lord Dunroe. He knows he is deceiving Sir Thomas who knows he is deceiving Lord Dunroe. Lucy is unaware of either man's perfidy. Just as the mumbling minister is about to perform the service, Lord Cullamore arrives and tells Sir Thomas that his children are illegitimate and the property belongs to his brother's son, the real Lord Dunroe who is Lucy's lover, Ensign Roberts.

Anthony Corbet announces he has much to reveal, for this is his hour of vengence. He informs the baronet that his supposed legitimate son is Corbet's bastard grandson. Corbet admits that Sir Thomas has hired him to kidnap his brother's son, but unknown to anyone, Corbet also kidnaps the son of Sir Thomas. In later years, he brings back the baronet's legitimate son as the son of his brother, following Lord Thomas's order to beat, chain, isolate, and starve the young man. Corbet calls Sam Roberts forward and states that Ensign Roberts is not his son but Lady Gourlay's son and heir to Red Hall. In time, Lord Dunroe marries Lucy and Sir Edward marries Emily.

Carleton indirectly discusses Ireland's problems, a country where parents feed upon the bodies of their children, explained in a footnote as alluding "to a dreadful fact of cannibalism which occurred in the South of Ireland in 1846" (*W*, 1:430). When writing about aristocrats, Carleton was somewhat similar to Anna Maria Hall, a middle-class Dubliner. Her *Sketches of Irish Character* (1829), *Lights and Shadows of Irish Life* (1838), *The Whiteboy* (1845), and *Stories of the Irish Peasantry* (1850), according to Carleton, were inferior works because she had never been intimate with country people. The reviewer of *Red Hall* in the *Athenaeum* (November 13, 1852) made a similar judgment about Carleton, noting that one cannot expect an artist who excels in depicting the passions and manners of the lower class to capture the frigid elegance of the upper class with its conventions.

Duffy, his publisher, told Carleton that *The Black Baronet* was "decidedly the best of all your works" (*L*, 2:239). O'Donoghue thought that evaluation was an exaggeration because the novel was "too melodramatic in tone, and the characters are not such as to enlist either the sympathy or the attention of the reader" (*L*, 2:240). Boué was not overly impressed by the novel and found the plot needlessly complicated, somewhat in the style of Wilkie Collins.[14]

There is merit in the tale in that Carleton demonstrates the demonic characteristics of humanity independent of class, using literary conventions: incognitos, masks, disguises, and a prolonged suspense. The novel is Carleton's most sophisticated work, written after an extensive planning period in which he worked out the many episodes to dovetail into the cohesive plot, proof that he could handle English and continental literary conventions. He also introduces characters representing Dubliners and Belfast acquaintances, unusual in the Carleton canon. The "Old Charlies," or Dublin police, and the city magistrates are sketched from life as is Sam Roberts who had for years given lessons on the use of the sword in Dublin schools. The effort Carleton exerted in *The Black Baronet* does not add anything to his reputation, but it demonstrates Carleton's desire to be recognized as more than a successful novelist of his own culture.

The Evil Eye or The Black Spectre and Redmond Count O'Hanlon, the Irish Rapparee, an Historical Tale

The next novel is a revision of "The Evil Eye" which appeared in John Mitchel's *Irish Tribune* (1848). It is Carleton's contribution to the Gothicism which Joseph Sheridan LeFanu after Maturin's death successfully revived in Ireland with *The House by the Churchyard* (1863) and *Uncle Silas* (1864). Carleton's *The Evil Eye or The Black Spectre* (1860) does not reach the same level of suspense that is found in LeFanu's works, nor are the characterizations as convincing because Carleton is not telling an original story. He sets the tale in seventeenth-century Ireland and dramatizes the exploits of a famous faith healer, Dr. Valentine Greatrakes of Waterford, against the background of the superstitious beliefs associated with the evil eye, the glance capable of inflicting harm. There is a strain in the novel between the natural and the supernatural worlds, and the reader is never sure of the author's intent. The country people obviously believe in the power of the evil eye, a universal folk belief, but Greatrakes confuses the point of the novel and detracts from the villainy of Woodward who has the power of the evil eye and uses it to destroy Alice Goodwin.

Carleton does not evoke the proper atmosphere for the tale, which could have been a thriller since it is manipulating a folk belief. There are a few good scenes: the description of the spa at Ballyspellan which people visit for their health is one and the Tory hunt when dispossessed tenants are hunted by bloodhounds is another. The heroic characterization of Charles Lindsay and Shawn na Middogue (John of the Dagger) is flat. The novel attempts to create a story that does not involve Carleton's immediate or past acquaintances, but by avoiding them, he fails to reproduce a credible theme. A French translation, *Le Mauvais Oeil ou le Spectre Noir* (1865) added to Carleton's reputation and attested to his popularity. The novel, republished in 1863, 1864, and 1880 in Dublin, was also published in America in 1875 and is included in *The Works of William Carleton* (1970).

Redmond Count O'Hanlon, earlier published as "The Rapparee" in *Duffy's Hibernian Magazine* (1860), is also set in the seventeenth century. Count O'Hanlon is the heroic protagonist who steals from the English settlers and gives to the Irish poor. He also avenges Irish injustices and has an honored reputation among the Irish. The novel is set in 1696, which is the period following the Battle of the Boyne and the Williamite settlement initiating the penal laws.

Actually, Count O'Hanlon operated several decades earlier and was captured and executed by William Lucas, a garrisoned English officer who hired an informer to betray O'Hanlon. Carleton's novel does not reproduce the harsh reality of the period when the Irish aristocracy, composed of Irish speakers most of whom were Catholic, was being replaced by the foreign land holders who became the nineteenth-century absentee landlords. There is more humor than tragedy in *Redmond Count O'Hanlon* wherein the main conflict between O'Hanlon's band of outlaws and Lucas's garrisoned soldiers concerns the recovery of Rose Callan, abducted for Lucas's pleasure. The outraged country people are helpless until O'Hanlon, a master of disguise, gets into the barracks and escapes with Rose. His band fights and defeats the soldiers, and the novel concludes with O'Hanlon dancing at Rose's wedding party. Duffy published a new edition in 1886, its last publication. One merit of the novel is its calling attention to Count O'Hanlon and the fall of the Irish aristocracy.

Chapter Six
The Autobiography

After a stressful life during which Carleton never lost his ambivalent feelings toward the Irish people, loving and damning them according to his mood, he began to write his autobiography in August 1868. The great writer was old, almost blind, and suffering from cancer of the tongue. The physical pain was compounded by the emotional trauma of sadly watching his sons' preparation for their emigration to New Zealand, a repetition of his eldest son William's emigration to Australia. Carleton was further distressed by the knowledge that his wife and spinster daughters Mary Anne and Jane would be destitute after his death when his pension would cease.

Considering his physical and emotional distress, one marvels at the vigor and lightheartedness of *The Autobiography* (1896). He dictated it with difficulty to his daughters or wrote almost illegibly on a slate for their rewriting. Deprived of vision and speech, the renowned storyteller struggled to narrate the story of a life marked with great successes and failures over seventy-five years of a tumultuous period in Irish history. Carleton's own story, unpublished until O'Donoghue rescued and edited it for publication almost thirty years later during the Irish literary revival, reveals how little he had in common with Griffin and the Banims. Both John Banim (1798–1842) and his brother Michael (1796–1874) were well-educated sons of a Kilkenny merchant farmer, and they retained their Catholicism. Gerald Griffin (1803–40) was from Limerick and well-educated, having studied law in London before joining the Catholic order of the Christian Brothers in Dublin. Carleton was a poorly educated member of the Catholic minority in the "black North" with its Protestant Scotch-Irish heritage, whereas the Banims and Griffin were heirs to the old Irish aristocratic culture, predominantly Catholic, preserved in Munster.

Carleton, as a Catholic Ulsterman, experienced pain and a

sense of inferiority because the dominant Protestant culture persecuted and belittled him. Like his father and many Catholic farmers, Carleton shunned politics for he could not imagine himself a political leader or a patriot who could bring about the necessary reform to allow Catholic Irishmen to become politicians. The episodes in *The Autobiography* clearly demonstrate his apolitical nature. His last literary contribution to nineteenth-century literature consisted of re-creating the mass culture of late eighteenth-century and early nineteenth-century rural and urban Ireland. Carleton spoke powerfully to the twentieth century, Yeats certainly listened, and talked of the changes that radically altered the political, economic, and social character of Ireland. Carleton knew his age was over and that it had not been replaced by a better one. *The Autobiography,* written during the lull in Irish literature when the great writers were dead and the famous generation of the Irish literary revival were being born, marked the end of one age and the beginning of another.

Today, Carleton's humble story reads like an odyssey of the human spirit. The nineteen chapters of his life present a picture of his parents who lived through the penal age, and his birth, early childhood, adolescence, and manhood in the Clogher Valley. Carleton also candidly discusses his wandering years prior to his arrival in Dublin, his marriage, association with the Sunday School Society, and teaching at Mullingar and Carlow. The tale begins with a description of the cottage in which he was born and ends with a description of his house in Carlow; the former is a better residence. Of the nineteen chapters, twelve are devoted to his early life and travels, disclosing the old man's fascination with his lost youth. The other seven chapters depict Dublin, its low and high characters, and his observations about them before he departs with his wife and daughter Mary Anne for Mullingar. He looks at the Clogher Valley and the countryside north of Dublin as images beneath which there is a substructure of meaning that he understands, but on seeing Dublin, the rustic artist views a metropolitan region about which he knows nothing. Carleton lived in Dublin with memories of his innocent youth, recollected in his fiction and revitalized in *The Autobiography.*

In his seventy-fifth year, the infirm old man wrote as though he were reliving the early years, reunited with his family and friends after a lifetime of suffering. That youthful spirit in no small measure accounts for the vitality of his story, which, according to Frances Cashel Hoey in her introduction, whets the reader's curiosity "with its gusto of simple ignorance of man and things on certain lines, its fine intensity, its frank unapologetic vanity."[1] O'Donoghue, who completes Carleton's story, thinks the autobiography illustrates "a great genius, an undisciplined temperament; a man of many moods and faults . . . of whom his countrymen will always be proud, although he vexed them sorely" (*L*, 1:X). By retaining a persistently optimistic attitude during the dictation and writing of his own story, Carleton demonstrates the better aspect of his personality. He expresses his hunger for social comforts in an ordered society, giving the impression that he is still standing outside its magic circle, less in the posture of contemptuous rejection or heroic defiance and more in the posture of woeful acceptance and a final awareness that some personality quirk made him an outcast in Clogher and Dublin.

An explication of a chapter from the Clogher phase and another from the early Dublin years sufficiently reveals the literary value of a work which at first may seem to be a simplistic apology. Chapter 9, which talks of the last episodes in Clogher, and Chapter 18, which treats of his tentative teaching tenure in Mullingar, represent these two phases of Carleton's life. He is the genuine hero of *The Autobiography*. Chapter 9 begins with the breakup of his family. Poking fun at his brother John's hypochondria, Carleton says, "He never imagined himself well, and persisted in drinking an extraordinary variety of herbal drugs" (*L*, 1:108). When James, who never married, also moves with Carleton and their mother to their married sister's cottage, it signals the loss of Carleton's home. In explaining the breakup, he does so by remembering one of his athletic feats. He and James bring twelve sacks of oats to Clogher Mill to be dried and ground. There he encounters the miller Frank Farrell, a huge man. Carleton's old descriptive powers are used to identify Frank, a kind, quiet, rather sluggish person without great courage or spirit to match his physical strength. Then the quick dialogue between Carleton and Farrell discloses the nature of their contest: the throwing of a fifty-pound weight over the beam of the aged building, "white with mealy cobwebs."

The young author, unbeaten in any athletic event that season, feels the urge to compete. James and a half dozen men try to dissuade him from attempting the feat, which only makes it seem more worthwhile. Carleton admits that pointing out difficulties to him forces him to try to overcome them. In the mill, he announces that he will attempt the throw, and the word goes through the village. A crowd gathers, which gratifies and encourages him, and he successfully throws the weight over the beam. "I can truthfully assert that I derive more gratification from the limited fame . . . than ever I did from that won by my success in literature. This I think every rational reader will understand" (*L*, 1:109). His judgment about athletics and literature may not be shared by all rational readers, but it indicates the low esteem in which he places the literary public and the high esteem he gives to the friends of his youth. In passing, he mentions Frank Farrell's part in "The Battle of the Factions" and his accidental death in repairing the Clogher Cathedral.

Going back to his own story, Carleton confesses he leads an erratic existence without a permanent home, living with friends and relatives, lacking an attainable goal, and being hounded for his idleness by his brother Michael with whom he resides for a few months. Carleton now remembers Michael's voice with its "low, gnawing, bitter, sneering spirit," but earlier Michael and James receive money and gifts from Carleton. In a letter to his cousin John Carleton on December 8, 1843, the author says the government will soon grant his pension (actually given in 1848), and he intends to visit Clogher: "The strongest wish of my heart is to see my native place, and my own dear friends—*but*—and mark that *but*—I shall not return to my native place until I am able to take my brothers, John, James, and Michael, out of their present poverty" (*L*, 2:63). Michael's inaccurate characterization results from his failure to appreciate his younger brother's talents, a grievous shortcoming, in Carleton's opinion.

Later in the chapter, Carleton corrects the error by saying it is Michael's love for him that makes him want to see William established in a trade. To please Michael, Carleton agrees to become an apprentice to a stonecutter, saying that if he is not accepted, he will enlist in the army. Meanwhile, he prepares for another athletic feat, a jump across a stream that has never been jumped before. A crowd assembles at the appointed hour, but Carleton, so depressed at the sight of himself dressed in an apron and cap no better than the workingmen in the audience, becomes listless, loses courage, and admits he cannot make the jump. Then he changes his mind and drinks some whiskey to raise his spirits. Knowing he can jump and feeling like walking on air, Carleton makes a run and glides over the stream, his last feat in Clogher Valley. Remembering the cheers of the crowd, he proudly says that to this day, the spot is called "Carleton's Leap," part of the local folklore.[2]

Carleton's future apprenticeship weighs so heavily upon him that he feels bitterness and hatred for the world. The misanthropy arises from his family's poverty and the dreaded capitulation to "shapeless granite," the chisel, and the mallet. He contemplates suicide, but overcomes that notion. To delay the apprenticeship, he visits his father's brother and family, who are engaged in the production of linen cloth at the nearby town of Skelgy. William accompanies his cousins every evening to the dancing school run by Buckramback. Bragging a bit, the dying Carleton says that at jigs, reels, and hornpipes, he beat the master. There is hardly a dance he does not learn. The vision of the dancing master, a rebel of '98 and a drummer who deserted so many times from the army that his back is cartilaginous from floggings, intrigues Carleton. He says the dapper little fellow teaches quadrilles, waltzes, and fashionable dances unknown to the country people.

Buckramback's fiddler is blind Mickey McRory, a humorous man acquainted with a wide range of Irish music, which he played on his violin. Carleton identifies him as the fiddler at his brother John's wedding, dramatized in "Shane Fadh's Wedding," *Traits and Stories,* and "Mickey McRory, the Irish Fiddler," *Irish Penny Journal.* Updating his interest in McRory, the author mentions that the literary portrait has made the fiddler's fortune, for he had been unable to meet a tenth of his requests. Carleton also mentions that six months ago, a newspaper recorded McRory's death at about ninety years of age and alluded to Carleton's selection of the fiddler as a model of his class. The aspiring author is enjoying Buckramback, McRory, and the hospitable Carletons whom he informs of his apprenticeship. They are indignant and shame Willy out of his engagement. Weeks pass and the 'prentice lad does not appear at home. He is practicing quadrilles and waltzes under Buckramback who finds him an apt pupil, but the dancing days cannot last forever. He returns to Michael's home and awaits his brother's condemnation. Briefly and decisively, Michael tells William to leave and open a dancing school. Carleton leaves Michael and the Clogher Valley, but retaining vivid memories of his life there.

Chapter 18 opens with Carleton asking for a job from Dr. Wilson who keeps an approved list of schoolmasters for the Protestant clergy. An interview is arranged between Carleton and Abraham Newland who runs a Dublin school and is looking for a teacher for his son's church school in Mullingar. Recalling that interview, Carleton says Newland is unimpressed and treats him like a servant looking for a domestic position. The dialogue between Newland and Carleton quickly changes that impression, and he establishes his classical reputation. "I believe it is admitted that I am a classical scholar, sir" (*L*, 1:267). Newland apologizes and tells Carleton he will write to his son Henry, notifying him of Carleton's qualifications.

Carleton exposes the painful raw nerve of his humble birth that controls much of his behavior. He demands to be treated like a gentleman because of his classical knowledge, which he wears as a badge of pride identifying his extraordinary escape from ignorance. As he travels by the canal route from Dublin to Mullingar, he anticipates a gentleman's welcoming committee. He is pleased when Henry Newland meets him at the canal station operated by a man past ninety. Carleton's wife and daughter are taken to their lodgings, and he joins Newland and other gentlemen from Tullamore at dinner, satisfying a need to establish himself as a gentleman in the new setting.

On confronting the nature of his teaching assignment, the pleasant feelings fade, being replaced by a deep melancholy. The school consists of one room on the upper floor of his lodgings, and his sixteen or eighteen students are as uncultured and wretched looking as his former students in Newcastle. Ready to quit and look for something else, he is reminded by his wife, who is not yet nineteen years old, that they have food and shelter which many other families do not have; she urges him to withhold his judgment. Thus, Jane Carleton's more mature nature checks her husband's impulsiveness, and she tells him to wait and see how things develop rather than give up on his first teaching day. Reluctantly, he follows her advice while commenting on the sad fact that he is forced to stay in order to earn their livelihood. His exaggerated sense of importance and his distaste for work beneath his dignity is a disturbing facet of his personality. Jane impresses him with her excellent business sense, and he wonders where she acquired such understanding since she has not endured his struggles. Carleton does not realize that he has not learned from his experiences, which were based on his unstable temperament and irrational expectations. Jane assumes an important role in making his dream of being a gentleman come true.

The schoolmaster, getting over his initial distaste for his appointment, begins his assignment, but in two months, he loses Jane's help as she gives birth to their daughter Jane, the second of their ten children. As the number of students increase, a larger room in a damp smelly old house is used, and Carleton objects to it: "I never felt such a detestable and abhorrent change" (L, 1:267). He agrees to stay because a new schoolhouse and residence for the schoolmaster is planned. On reminiscing about Mullingar, he recalls two interesting events: first, the romance of the ninety-four-year-old canal stationmaster and an attractive, quiet, sensible nineteen-year-old village girl. Despite his age, the healthy old man works daily, has not a wrinkle in his face or a white hair on his head, and is mentally alert; he shocks the townspeople by marrying the young girl. They are struck dumb when nine months later, his wife is delivered of a son who is the image of his father. The sensational family receives gifts for months after the birth. To satisfy his curiosity, Carleton visits the couple and reports the astonishing resemblance between the newborn and his father.

The second event concerns the Ninety-Third Scotch Regiment, which is quartered a short distance from Mullingar and has a hostile relationship with the townspeople. Carleton's relationship with the soldiers, however, is a cordial one, and he often spends evenings with the parents of his students. He walks to the barracks, engages the librarian in conversation, and borrows books from him. Most of the townsmen do not share Carleton's sympathy and make the soldiers feel unwelcome. They are often beaten on their walks to and from the town, and one young soldier is murdered near the canal without a clue to his murderer. Within a month or so after the inquest, everything settles down until one evening when the enraged Scots, seeking revenge, storm out of the barracks. Armed with heavy cudgels, they separate into two groups to attack the people. Hardly expecting a raid from the soldiers stationed to maintain the peace, the frightened townspeople think the Ribbonmen have come to burn the town but learn that the furious soldiers are attacking all the civilians they meet along their route.

Once the citizens are knocked down, the furious men club them into insensibility with their heavy cudgels. Windows are smashed, bodies are strewn about the streets, and people who open their doors to investigate the attack are beaten and thrown inside the house or dragged outside screaming and clubbed until quiet. William Kidd, the proprietor of the *Westmeath Guardian* who has been standing near the office door, is hit several times on the head and almost killed. Carleton on hearing the noise runs outside into the path of three violent men. They go after him and would have beaten him but for a voice shouting, "Hauld your hauns—that gentleman disna belong to them" (*L*, 1:273). The soldiers retreat and Carleton recognizes the librarian who tells him to get back into his house. Once their anger is spent, the soldiers return to the barracks, and the people pick up their fallen friends and family members. Mullingar for almost a month is like a hospital as it tries to restore normalcy; it complains to the War Office which investigates and removes the regiment from the town. This decision, according to Carleton, is like a man cutting off his nose to spite his face because the Ninety-Third Regiment is a financial asset to the community. Other people think differently and hold a triumphant banquet when the soldiers leave. The chapter ends with Carleton's observation that the loss of the regiment becomes a standing joke among the citizens.

The Autobiography continues with Carleton asking for a transfer from Mullingar after Newland leaves the parish. In the meanwhile, Carleton takes over the finances of the school, and the first thing he does is to rent a larger, more comfortable house for his school and residence. One evening after a social meeting with the "most respectable" citizens, two bailiffs approach Carleton to arrest him for debt. One man punches Carleton's shoulder, and he explodes, knocking them both down. A friend convinces him to go quietly with the men to jail, which he does. At this juncture Carleton says, "I must say that there was a good deal of dramatic incident in my life" (*L*, 1:283). He then describes his jail experiences, his release, and his return to Dublin where he is reassigned to a school in Carlow.

From the first until the last chapter of *The Autobiography*, Carleton is on stage, playing a heroic role. Since he was writing, directing, and selecting incidents for the drama, the author was in full control of his production. He did not withhold unpleasant information from his Protestant daughters who were recording his story. They faithfully preserved the manuscript which describes his love and abiding affection for his parents and family, praising their religious sentiments, piety, and loyalty to Catholicism. Because of Mary Anne and Jane Carleton, one knows of their father's attachment to Anne Duffy and in 1846 his visiting her in the desolate Clogher Valley where only her home stood among the many that formerly lined the roadside. They also retained Carleton's final statements about the Protestant and Catholic clergy. Looking back at the battles within the established Anglican church with its two diametrically opposed parties, Carleton wonders about the bitter feelings generated on both sides over unimportant trifles. From the Mullingar jail cell shared with a defrocked Catholic priest incarcerated for performing a marriage between a Catholic and Protestant, Carleton makes his final judgment of priests. They are, he believes, the most moral class of men on God's earth and their fall from grace is a terrible maddening descent which fills their minds with an incredible recklessness and indecency. The most outrageous behavior is a sign of the internal torture they suffer. The insights that Carleton revealed months before his death were an expression of his psyche at rest. He no longer had to please anyone but his artistic self which surfaced on taking the long look backward, back to the culture that molded him and held him.

One important reason why *The Autobiography,* which Patrick Kavanagh calls Carleton's "lost world of ambition and deprivation,"[3] is a magnificent literary accomplishment is its absolute candor. It forces the reader to gaze upon this man's restless pursuit of knowledge and understanding of man's relationship with man. Religious dogma meant little to Carleton who was captivated by men, women, and children in whom he expected to find the divine spark. He simplistically expected people to do the right thing and took offense if they did not. He candidly explains how he endured the evictions, the emigration of his children to whom he is the most affectionate of fathers, the small and the great famines, the financial distress, and his final illness.

Carleton's indomitable spirit has a touch of the ancient poet's character, which he reminds his reader. Carleton honestly tells his final audience that he has never accepted the contradictions of his life, has never had to release his soul from confinement or restrain his zest for life. When he had to choose between the stonecutter and Buckramback, he chose the artist. He could not live with a hammer during the day and a feathered pen at night, nor could he understand why a man is forced to make such a decision. Without apologizing for his life, Carleton apologizes for the lack of charity in a Christian Irish society which forced people to make irrational choices that could kill the human spirit. He is saying that no one with his talents should ever have suffered as he did. During the periods of his most intense pain, he is free to behave as outrageously and shamelessly as a fallen priest, expecting people to love him despite his actions. The philosophical force that flows through *The Autobiography* and brings all the streams of Carleton's thoughts into a mighty river is his equation of spirit with humanity. His last work, a realistic story of a romantic man's life which is so fused with his art that it is difficult to separate the two, remains an excellent work of art as well as spirit.

Notes and References

Chapter One

1. Following Theobald Wolfe Tone's founding of the Society of United Irishmen in 1791, Catholic voting rights and a lessening of English political power in Ireland were demanded. See Justin H. McCarthy, *Ireland since the Union* (London: Chatto and Windus, 1887), pp. 38–56, for an overview of the secret urban and rural organizations preying upon each other and the Dublin government's paid informers in the Society of the United Irishmen.

2. See Gilbert A. Cahill's "The Irish Parliamentary Tradition— Past and Present," *Conflict in Ireland,* ed. Eileen A. Sullivan and Harold A. Wilson (Gainesville, Fla.: Renaissance Print & Publishing, 1976), pp. 73–85, for an account of the political power of the Orange Lodges and its support by English lords and the Hierarchy of the Anglican church in England and Ireland; hereafter cited as *Conflict.*

3. Daniel Corkery in *The Hidden Ireland* (Dublin: Gill, 1967), p. 127, suggests that Irish art in the eighteenth century consisted only of literature and music because they were "arts that require little or no gear."

4. William Carleton states in *Traits and Stories of the Irish Peasantry,* (London, 1852), p. viii, that his father knew "all kinds of charms, old ranns of poems, old prophecies, religious superstitions, tales of pilgrimages, and revelations from ghosts and fairies."

5. The Union of 1801 solved England's immediate problem, but according to P. S. O'Hegarty in *A History of Ireland under the Union, 1801–1922* (London: Methuen, 1952), p. 5: "It uncovered much more formidable danger. It uncovered the Underground Nation. They had no rights that could be destroyed, because all rights had been destroyed. . . . And they were coming out, out of the darkness of the eighteenth century, out into the light, with their long memory, their steadfast purpose, their endurance, their persistence, out to the attack."

6. William Carleton in *The Life of William Carleton*, 2 vols. (London, 1896), 1:29, states that "there was then no law *against* an Orangeman and no law *for* a Papist." Volume 1 was written by Carleton and Volume 2 by David O'Donoghue; hereafter cited in text as *L*.

7. Steven Emery in "Influence of Old Irish Beliefs on Carleton," *Carleton Newsletter* 2, no. 4 (April 4, 1972):30, makes an interesting association between Carleton's dream and the ancient Irish ritual of *tairbfheis*, or "bull-sleep," a divination rite whereby an individual acquires knowledge from the deity.

8. Daniel J. Casey reconstructed the accounts of the eight murders of October 30, 1816. See "Wildgoose Lodge: The Evidence and the Lore," pt. I, *County Louth Archaelogical and Historical Journal* 18, no. 2 (1974):140–64; hereafter cited as *CLAHJ*.

9. Carleton states in "A Pilgrimage to Patrick's Purgatory," *Christian Examiner* 6:271, that he was in the "middle of my nineteenth year—of quick perception—warm imagination—a mind peculiarly romantic—a morbid turn for devotion."

10. See Eileen S. Ibarra's "William Carleton and the Picaresque Novel: The Irish Peasant and the Spanish Picaro," *Carleton Newsletter* 1 no. 4 (April 4, 1971):27.

11. In "Wildgoose Lodge: The Evidence and the Lore," pt. 2, *CLAHJ* 17, no. 4 (1975):211–31, Casey traces the influence of Carleton's "Wildgoose Lodge" on the local folklore of the murders.

12. Gordon W. Allport in *The Individual and His Religion* (New York: Macmillan, 1971), p. 32, states that the child's first religious responses are not religious but social, routine acts required by parents.

13. Letter of Carleton to William Sisson, British Museum, Mss. 40 390, Peel papers, vol. CCS, 29–35. Cited In André Boué's *William Carleton, 1794–1869, Romancier Irlandais* (Irish Novelist) (Université de Lille III, 1973), pp. 495–98.

14. Stephen Gwynn, *A Student's History of Ireland* (London: Macmillan, 1925), p. 215.

15. J. C. Beckett, *A Short History of Ireland* (London: Hutchinson's University Library, 1958), p. 150.

16. André Boué, *William Carleton*, p. 112.

Chapter Two

1. William Carleton, *The Works of William Carleton*, 2 vols. (New York, 1970), 2:797. Facsimile of Collier's 1880 edition of two

volumes, incorrectly identified as Collier's 1881 edition of three volumes; hereafter cited in text as *W*.

2. Boué, *William Carleton*, p. 121.

3. Benedict Kiely, *Poor Scholar* (New York, 1948), p. 88.

4. Daniel Casey in "Lough Derg's Infamous Pilgrim," *Carleton Newsletter* 3, no. 1 (July 4, 1972):2–8, has analyzed the two versions and noted the nine omissions in the later version and stylistic differences between the two tales.

5. Margaret Chesnutt, *Studies in the Short Stories of William Carleton*, Gothenberg Studies in English, 34 (Goteborg, 1976), p. 30.

6. Thomas Flanagan, *The Irish Novelists: 1800–1850* (New York: Columbia University Press, 1959), p. 281.

7. Carleton, *Christian Examiner* 6:269; hereafter cited in the text as *CE*.

8. The version in *Traits and Stories* (1833) is practically a different story because of the major deletions and additions. Several other versions also exist which include abridgements entitled "Going to Maynooth," and "The Irish Student or How the Protestant Church was Founded by Luther and the Devil." The story in *The Works of William Carleton* (1970) is still another variation that resembles the *Traits and Stories* version but does not include the comic addition that explains the establishment of Protestantism by Henry VIII and Martin Luther. The editions by David O'Donoghue (1896), Maurice Harmon (1973), and Eileen Sullivan (1974, 1975) are based on the corrected, annotated, and revised edition of *Traits and Stories* (1843–44) and contain the comic explanation and other additions, omitting the long proselytizing passages.

Superficial changes in the *Traits and Stories* version constitute numerous alterations in paragraph formation, punctuation, and spelling which includes Dennis becoming Denis. Deep changes are the deletion of about eight pages of the journal's edition and the increase from a 51-page manuscript to one of 137 pages (a journal page equals about three-quarters of a page in *Traits and Stories*). The new incidents include the foundation of the Protestant church, Denis's meetings with Susan Connor, and a different ending. The superficial and deep structural changes alter the tone and intention of the tale which converts the controversial religious propaganda to a comic Horatian satire about a mock-hero. Since the pedantic proud youth is in the author's image, Carleton turns the joke upon himself and exposes his faults, folly, ignorance, and aspirations without attacking the process by which rural men are trained for the Catholic priesthood or ridiculing their families who cherish such ambitions for their sons.

Because of the extensive changes, "Denis O'Shaughnessy" of *Traits and Stories* emerges as a far greater work than "Dennis O'Shaughnessy" of the *Christian Examiner.*

Chapter Three

1. In talking to the descendants of Carleton's literary characters in Clogher Valley, this author was told that their people did not know they were peasants until Carleton identified them as such.
2. Catholic and Protestant members of the Carleton Society in Ireland today look to "Ned M'Keown" for references to their ancestors.
3. See John Fair's "Londonderry, Enniskillen, and the Boyne: In the Defense of Ulster," *Conflict,* pp. 7–18.
4. John Wilson, *Blackwood's Magazine* 69 (May 1830):808.
5. See the reviews in *Athenaeum* (April 17 and 24, 1830), *Dublin Literary Magazine* (May and June 1830), and *National Magazine* (August 1830).
6. William Carleton, *Traits and Stories of the Irish Peasantry* (Philadelphia and Baltimore, 1833), p. vi.
7. J. Scott Porter in *The Catholic Religion of St. Patrick and St. Colum-Kill* (Belfast: Simms & McIntyre, 1845) pleads for the elimination of Catholicism because holy wells, decorated with thousands of rags, were dedicated to saints who had replaced pagan heroes.
8. Joseph Campbell, *Myths to Live By* (New York: Viking, 1972), p. 93.
9. William Carleton, *Tubber Derg, Denis O'Shaughnessy, Phelim O'Toole's Courtship, and Neal Malone* (Florida, 1974, 1975), p. 304.
10. Ibid., p. 305.
11. Ibid., p. 326.
12. Ibid., p. 316.
13. Ibid., p. 319.
14. Lucien Leclair, *Le Roman régionaliste dans les illes britanniques 1800–1850* (The Regional Novel in the British Isles), (Paris: Les Belles Lettres (Fine Literature), 1954), p. 51.
15. See Robert L. Meredith's "William Carleton and Charles Lever," *Carleton Newsletter* 3, no. 2 (October 4, 1972):11–15.
16. Louis James, *Fiction for the Working Man, 1830–1850* (London: Oxford University Press, 1963), p. 1.
17. William Carleton, *Tales and Sketches* (Dublin, 1845) p. 30. A

confusion in titles appears in this edition. The spine and first page identify the work as *Tales and Stories of the Irish Peasantry;* however, the second title page reads *Tales and Sketches Illustrating the Character, Usage, Traditions, Sports, and Pasttimes of the Irish Peasantry.* The work is usually identified as *Tales and Sketches.*

Chapter Four

1. Carleton, *Fardorougha the Miser* (Dublin, 1846), p. vii.
2. Carleton's unique creativity is often overlooked. Horatio Krans in *Irish Life in Irish Fiction* (New York: Columbia University Press, 1903), p. 316, said that Carleton is "without question, the creative genius among the Irish novelists."
3. "*Fardorougha the Miser*," *Athenaeum*, no. 613 (July 27, 1839), p. 563.
4. See Gearoid O'Tuathaigh's *Ireland before the Famine, 1798–1848* (Dublin: Gill & Macmillan, 1972).
5. George O'Brien in *The Economic History of Ireland from the Union to the Famine* (London; Longmans, Green & Co., 1921) analyzes the problem that existed between landlords and the various levels of land leasers.
6. Marilyn Butler in *Maria Edgeworth: A Literary Biography* (Oxford: Oxford University Press, 1972).
7. Francis Maurice Egan and Justin McCarthy, eds., *Irish Literature*, vol. 5 (Philadelphia: De Bower-Elliott, 1904), vii, say "His novels . . . must have an enormous sociological influence on the work of the future historians of Ireland."
8. William Carleton, *Valentine M'Clutchy* (Dublin, 1847), p. viii.
9. Ibid., p. x.
10. Ibid., p. xii.
11. Kiely, *Poor Scholar*, p. 111.
12. Carleton, *Valentine M'Clutchy* (Dublin, 1847), p. 132.
13. Ibid., p. 133.
14. Ibid., p. 67.
15. "*Valentine M'Clutchy*," *Athenaeum*, no. 898 (January 11, 1845), pp. 38–39.
16. Carleton, *The Black Prophet* (Dublin, 1972), p. 136.
17. Ibid., p. xi.
18. Ibid., p. vii.
19. James S. Donnelly, Jr., *Landlord and Tenant in Nineteenth Century Ireland* (Dublin: Gill & Macmillan, 1973), p. 44.

20. Ibid., p. 6.
21. Kiely, *Poor Scholar*, p. 172.
22. Ibid., p. 57.

Chapter Five

1. John Stuart Mill, *England and Ireland* (London: Longmans, Green & Co., 1868), p. 3, states that "short of actual depopulation and desolation, or the direct personal enslaving of the inhabitants, little was omitted which could give a people cause to execrate its conquerors."
2. Daniel O'Connell in an address to the people of Tipperary on September 30, 1828, said, "I advised you to give up factious fights and quarrels—you have given them up. I advised you to abstain from party feuds and riots—you have abstained from them." *The Memoirs, Private and Political of Daniel O'Connell,* ed. Robert Huish (London: W. Johnston, 1836), p. 331.
3. Stephen J. Brown, *Ireland in Fiction,* (London: Maunsel & Co., 1969), p. 56.
4. Flanagan, *The Irish Novelists,* p. 322.
5. Boué, *William Carleton,* p. 175.
6. William Bradley, *"The Tithe Proctor*—A Revaluation," *Carleton Newsletter* 3, no. 4 (April 4, 1973):30.
7. Duffy says that Carleton intended "to make it the foundation of a national novel, exhibiting the customs and prejudices of the unhappy world in which it is laid." Charles Gavan Duffy, *Ballad Poetry of Ireland* (Dublin: James Duffy, 1845), p. 112. The popular ballad known primarily in Ulster consisted of many versions which Carleton collated.
8. Boué, *William Carleton,* p. 190.
9. *Life,* 2:175.
10. Carleton, *The Squanders of Castle Squander* (London, 1876), p. 393.
11. Ibid., p. 356.
12. Kiely, *Poor Scholar*, p. 120.
13. Boué, *William Carleton,* p. 183.
14. Ibid., p. 183.

Chapter Six

1. Frances Cashel Hoey, *Life,* 1:xviii. Hoey was the wife of John Cashel Hoey, an editor of *Nation.*
2. Ibid., p. 119. The spot was still known as "Carleton's Leap" a decade ago when this author visited the Clogher Valley.

3.   Patrick Kavanagh, *The Autobiography of William Carleton* (London, 1968), p. 11. The flyleaf erroneously stated that Hoey, rather than David O'Donoghue, wrote Carleton's biography. The error is repeated in James Kilroy's "William Carleton," *The Dictionary of Irish Literature,* ed. Robert Hogan (Westport, Conn.: Greenwood, 1979).

Selected Bibliography

PRIMARY SOURCES

A complete authoritative edition of Carleton's works does not exist. The publication history of the short stories is particularly complex with different versions having the same title and different titles referring to the same story. Barbara Hayley of the Department of English at St. Patrick's College, Maynooth, County Kildare, Ireland, is compiling a bibliography for the Wolfhound Press, Dublin.

1. Short Stories
   a. Contributions to the *Christian Examiner:*
      "The Broken Oath," 6 (1828):27–39.
      "The Brothers,"10(1830):205–13, 287–96, 365–77, 440–52.
      "The Death of a Devotee," 9 (1829):267–83.
      "Dennis O'Shaughnessy Going to Maynooth," 11 (1831): 686–96, 765–79, 842–54, 930–45.
      "Father Butler,"7(1828):109–19, 192–202, 271–90, 355–65, 423–43.
      "History of a Chimney Sweep," 11 (1831):276–91.
      "The Illicit Distiller," 10 (1830):928–39.
      "Lachlin Murray and the Blessed Candle," 10 (1830):590–610.
      "The Lianhan Shee," 10 (1830):845–61.
      "The Materialist," 11 (1831):512–32.
      "A Pilgrimage to Patrick's Purgatory,"6(1828):268–86, 343–62.
      "The Priest's Funeral," 10 (1830):41–51, 128–42.
      "The Station," 8 (1829):45–60, 259–69, 422–38.
   b. Other Stories:
      "Alley Sheridan." *National Magazine* 1, no. 5 (1830).
      "Barney Brady's Goose." *Dublin University Magazine,* May 1838.
      "Black and All Black, a Legend of the Padereen Mare." *Illustrated London News* 17, no. 461 (December 1850).

"Bob Pentland or The Gauger Outwitted." *Irish Penny Journal,* no. 16 (1840).

"The Castle of Aughentain or The Legend of the Brown Goat, a Tale of Tom Gressiey, the Shanahus." *Irish Penny Journal,* no. 49 (1841).

"Condy Cullen or The Gauger Outwitted." In *The Irishman at Home, Characteristic Sketches.* Dublin: McGlashan, 1849.

"Confessions of a Reformed Ribbonman." *Dublin Literary Gazette* 1 (1830).

"The Country Dancing Master." *Irish Penny Journal,* no. 9 (1840).

"The Dead Boxer, an Irish Legend." *Dublin University Magazine* 2 (1833).

"Dick Magrath, a Sketch of Living Character." *Dublin Family Magazine,* no. 5 (1829).

"The Donagh or The Horse Stealers." *National Magazine* 1, no. 6 (1830).

"The Double Prophecy or Trials of the Heart." *Duffy's Hibernian Magazine,* January-September 1861.

"The Dream of a Broken Heart." *Dublin University Review and Quarterly Magazine* 1, no. 2, (1833).

"The Evil Eye." *Irish Tribune,* June 10, 17, and 24, 1848. It differs from the novel published in 1860.

"The Fair of Emyvale." *Illustrated London Magazine,* 1853.

"Fair Gurtha or The Hungry Grass." *Dublin University Magazine,* April 1856.

"The Foster Brother." *Irish Penny Journal,* no. 43 (1841).

"The Irish Fiddler." *Irish Penny Journal,* no. 7 (1840).

"The Irish Matchmaker." *Irish Penny Journal,* no. 15 (1840).

"The Irish Midwife." *Irish Penny Journal,* nos. 26, 27 (1840–41).

"The Irish Prophecy Man." *Irish Penny Journal,* no. 50 (1841).

"The Irish Shanahus." *Irish Penny Journal,* no. 48 (1841).

"Irish Superstitions—Ghosts and Fairies." *Irish Penny Journal,* no. 21 (1840).

"Irish Superstitions—Ghosts and Fairies, the Rival Kempers." *Irish Penny Journal,* no. 24 (1840).

"Irish Superstitions—No. III Ghosts and Fairies." *Irish Penny Journal,* no. 34 (1841).

"The King's Thief." *Commercial Journal and Family Herald*
(Dublin), September 22, 29, and October 6, 13,
1855.

"The Landlord and Tenant, an Authentic Story." *National
Magazine* 2, no. 10 (1831).

"Laying a Ghost." *National Magazine* 2, no. 7 (1831).

"A Legend of Knockmany." *Chambers' Edinburgh Journal*, no.
468 (January 16, 1841).

"The Man with the Black Eye." *Duffy's Hibernian Magazine*,
July 1860.

"Master and Scholar." *Illustrated London Magazine*, 1854.

"The Master of Mohill." *Illustrated Dublin Journal*, nos. 1–4
(September 1861).

"Neal Malone." *Dublin University Review and Quarterly Magazine* 1, no. 1 (1833).

"Ned M'Keown," "The Three Tasks," "Confessions of a
Reformed Ribbonman," "Neal Malone," "Tubber
Derg," "The Poor Scholar," and "The Two Brothers." In *Shamrock Leaves*. Boston: Patrick Donohoe,
1854.

"O'Sullivan's Love, a Legend of Edenmore." *Dublin University
Magazine*, March-April 1847.

"A Record of the Heart." *Citizen* 8, (June 1840).

"Richard the Rake." *Dublin University Magazine*, March
1838.

"The Romance of Instinct." *Shamrock* (Dublin), February
1869.

"The Silver Acre." *Illustrated London Magazine*, 1853–54.

"The Three Tasks." *Dublin Literary Gazette* 1 (1830).

"The Three Wishes." *Dublin University Magazine*, November
1839.

"Utrum Horum? or the Revenge of Shane Roe na Soggarth."
Dublin University Magazine, May-June 1860.

"The Weird Woman of Tavniemore or The Milking of the
Tethers, a Tale of Witchcraft." *Shamrock* (Dublin), April
1868.

c. Story Collections:

Alley Sheridan and Other Stories. Dublin: P. Dixon Hardy,
1857.

Amusing Irish Tales. London: Hamilton, Adams, & Co.,
1889.

The Battle of the Factions and Other Tales of Ireland. Philadelphia:
Carey & Hart, 1845.

Carleton's Stories of Irish Life. Introduction by Darrell Figgis. London: Talbot Press, 1918.

The Clarionet, the Dead Boxer, and Barney Branagan. London: Routledge, 1850.

The Courtship of Phelim O'Toole. Edited by Anthony Cronin. London: New English Library, 1962.

Dennis O'Shaughnessy Going to Maynooth. London: Routledge, 1845.

Denis O'Shaughnessy Going to Maynooth. Introduction by Maurice Harmon. Cork: Mercier Press, 1973.

Father Butler or Sketches of Irish Manners. Philadelphia: T. Laminer, 1834, 1835.

The Party Fight and Funeral. Cork: Mercier Press, 1973.

Phelim O'Toole's Courtship and Other Stories. Cork: Mercier Press, 1973.

Stories from Carleton. Introduction by W. B. Yeats. London: W. G. Gage, 1889.

Stories from Carleton. Facsimile of 1889 edition. New York: Lemma Publishers, 1977.

Tales and Sketches Illustrating the Character, Usages, Traditions, Sports, and Pasttimes of the Irish Peasantry. Dublin: James Duffy, 1845.

Traits and Stories of the Irish Peasantry, 1st series. Dublin: Wm. Curry, 1830, 1832.

Traits and Stories of the Irish Peasantry, 2nd series. Dublin: W. F. Wakeman, 1833, 1834, 1835.

Traits and Stories of the Irish Peasantry. 1st complete edition in monthly parts. Dublin: Wm. Curry, 1842–43.

Traits and Stories of the Irish Peasantry. Introduction by William Carleton. Illustrations by Harvey, Phiz, Franklin, MacManus, Gilbert, et. al. Dublin: Wm. Curry; London: W. S. Orr, 1843–44.

Tubber Derg, Denis O'Shaughnessy, Phelim O'Toole's Courtship, and Neal Malone. Introduction by Eileen A. Sullivan. Florida: Renaissance Printing, 1974, 1975.

2. Poems

"Farewell." *Nation,* December 1858.

"Jane Anderson, My Joe." *Life* 2 (1896):194–95.

"The Midnight Hour." *Christian Examiner,* November 1828.

"The Retrospect." *Dublin Family Magazine,* August 1829.

"Retrospections." *Christian Examiner,* September 1828.

"A Sigh for Knockmany." *National Magazine,* April 1831.

"Sir Turlough or The Churchyard Bride." *National Magazine,*
November 1830.
"A Song of Sorrow." *Dublin University Magazine,* September
1834.
"Taedet me Vitae." *Nation,* December 1854.

3. Drama
Irish Manufacture or Bob Gawley's Project. Presented on March 25,
1841, at the Theatre Royal, Dublin.

4. Novels
The Black Baronet or The Chronicles of Ballytrain. Dublin: James
Duffy, 1857, 1858, 1875.
The Black Prophet, a Tale of Irish Famine. London and Belfast:
Simms & McIntyre, 1847.
The Black Prophet. Introduction by D. J. O'Donoghue. Illustrations
by J. B. Yeats. London: Lawrence & Bollen, 1899.
The Black Prophet. Introduction by Timothy Webb. Photolitho-
graphic facsimile of 1899 edition. Shannon: Irish University
Press, 1972.
The Emigrants of Ahadarra, a Tale of Irish Life. London and Belfast:
Simms & McIntyre, 1847.
The Evil Eye or The Black Spectre. Dublin: James Duffy, 1860, 1863,
1864, 1880.
Fardorougha the Miser or The Convicts of Lisnamona. Dublin: Wm.
Curry, 1839, 1841.
Fardorougha the Miser or The Convicts of Lisnamona. Edited by
Robert Lee Wolff. Facsimile of 1839 edition. New York and
London: Garland Press, 1979.
The Fawn of Springvale. Dublin: Wm. Curry, 1841, 1843.
"A New Pyramus and Thisbe, the Battle of Aughrim." (From the
unpublished novel, "Ann Cosgrave"). *Blackwood's Edinburgh
Magazine,* 179 (February 1906).
The Red-Haired Man's Wife. Dublin: Sealy, Bryers, & Walker.
London: Simpkin & Marshall, 1889.
Red Hall or The Baronet's Daughter. Revised as *The Black Baronet.*
London: Saunders & Otley, 1852.
Redmond Count O'Hanlon, the Irish Rapparee, an Historic Tale.
Dublin: James Duffy, 1862, 1886.
The Squanders of Castle Squander. London: Illustrated London
Library, 1852.
The Tithe Proctor, a Novel, Being a Tale of the Tithe Rebellion

in Ireland. London and Belfast: Simms & McIntyre, 1849.

Valentine M'Clutchy, the Irish Agent or The Chronicles of the Castle Cumber Property. Dublin: James Duffy, 1845, 1846.

Willy Reilly and His Dear Colleen Bawn, a Tale Founded upon Fact. London: Hope & Co., 1855.

5. Autobiography
  The Life of William Carleton. Vol. 1. London: Downey, 1896.
  The Autobiography of William Carleton. Preface by Patrick Kavanagh. London: McGibbon & Kee, 1968.

6. Collected Works
  The Works of William Carleton. New York: Collier, 1880, 1881.
  The Works of William Carleton. New York: Books for Libraries Press, 1970.

SECONDARY SOURCES

Baker, Ernest A. "The Irish Novelists." In *The History of the English Novel.* Vol. 7. London: H. F. & G. Witherby, Ltd., 1936. Recognizes Carleton's talents.

Barbash, Nancy Eyles. "Violence in the Fiction of William Carleton." *Carleton Newsletter* 4, no. 3 (January 4, 1974):20–23. Demonstrates the social violence beneath the melodrama and sensationalism.

Bell, Sam Hanna. "William Carleton and His Neighbours." *Ulster Folklife,* no. 7 (1961), pp. 37–40. Sees Carleton's life and character reappearing in his fiction.

"The Black Prophet." *Athenaeum,* no. 1011 (March 13, 1847), pp. 278–79. Chides Carleton for exaggerating the famine suffering. Thought Darby Skinadre, the miser, helped the people by having grain to sell.

Boué, André. *William Carleton, 1794–1869, Romancier Irlandais* [Irish Novelist]. Lille: Université de Lille III, 1973. Presents a biographic sketch with a critical analysis of the short stories and novels. Excellent work.

Bradley, William. "The Scope and Quality of William Carleton's Presentation of Irish Peasant Life and Character in His Novels and Stories." MA. thesis, University of London,

1974. Documents Carleton's use of Irish country life for themes.

————. "The Tithe Proctor—Revaluation." *Carleton Newsletter* 3, no. 4 (April 4, 1973):28–30. Akin to current Northern Ireland violence.

Brown, Malcolm. *The Politics of Irish Literature from Thomas Davis to W. B. Yeats.* Seattle: University of Washington Press, 1972. Excellent study of the relationship between Irish literature and politics. Carleton is rare English writer who knew the country people, a blood brother to Tolstoy and Turgenev.

Brown, Terence. "The Death of William Carleton." *Hermathena* 110 (1970):81–85. New insight on Carleton's death. Reprinted in *Carleton Newsletter* 2, no. 2 (October 4, 1971): 12–13.

Bryson, Mary. "John Eglinton and William Carleton: The Search for a Prose Model for the Irish Literary Revival." *Carleton Newsletter* 5, no. 1 (October 4, 1974):4–6. Discusses John Eglinton's recognition of Carleton's role as the prose model for literary revival writers.

Buckley, Mary. "Attitudes to Nationalism in Four Ninteenth-Century Irish Novelists." M.A. thesis, University College, Cork, Ireland, 1973. A historical analysis of nationalism in work of Edgeworth, Carleton, Lever, and Hall.

Casey, Daniel. "Carleton in Louth." *County Louth Archaeological and Historical Journal.* 17, no. 2 (1970):96–106. A carefully researched account of Carleton's time in Louth, the locale of "Wildgoose Lodge."

————. "Carleton and Devaun." *Carleton Newsletter* 1 (January 4, 1971):19-22. A comparison of Carleton's Patrick Devaun in "Wildgoose Lodge" with the historical Devaun.

————. "Lough Derg's Infamous Pilgrim." *Clogher Record* 7, no. 3 (1971):449–64. A textual analysis of "A Pilgrimage to Patrick's Purgatory" with "The Lough Derg Pilgrim."

————. "Lough Derg's Infamous Pilgrim." *Carleton Newsletter* 3 (July 4, 1972):2–8. An edited version of the above.

————. "Wildgoose Lodge: The Evidence and the Lore." Pt. 1. *County Louth Archaeological and Historical Journal* 18, no. 2 (1974):140–64.

————. "Wildgoose Lodge: The Evidence and the Lore." Pt. 2. *County Louth Archeaological and Historical Journal* 18, no. 4 (1975):211–31. Extensive research into the murders at Louth that Carleton manipulates for his "Wildgoose Lodge."

———. "Carleton and the Count. *Seancas Ard Mhacha* 8, no. 1 (1975–76):7–22. Excellent review of Carleton's imaginative account of Redmond Count O'Hanlon's career as an outlaw.

———. "Three Roads Out of Clogher." *Clogher Record* 10, no. 3 (1981):392–404. Recounts Carleton's struggles in leaving the Clogher Valley.

Chesnutt, Margaret. *Studies in the Short Stories of William Carleton.* Gothenburg Studies on English, 34. Goteborg, Sweden: University of Goteborg, 1976. Superficial analysis of religion and social structure found in early short stories.

Davis, Thomas. "Carleton's *Traits and Stories.*" *Nation,* October 12, 1844. Praises Carleton's fine characterization of actual country people.

Denman, C. George. "Carleton's Characterization of Women." *Carleton Newsletter* 1, no. 2 (October 4, 1970):10–11. Notes the nobility of women characters from the purity of the young women to the "robust vigor" of the older women.

Dumbleton, William. "Dramatic Qualities in Carleton's Fiction." *Carleton Newsletter* 4, no. 4 (April 4, 1974):27–31. Fresh look at the dramatic quality in *Traits and Stories* and *Valentine M'Clutchy.*

Eckley, Grace. "Paddy's Ruse and Anna's Revenge: Carleton's 'Essay on Irish Swearing.'" *Carleton Newsletter* 1, no. 1 (July 4, 1970):4. Sees similarity between Carleton's characters swearing on the "Law" Bible and Joyce's Anna Livia's swearing in *Finnegans Wake.*

Emery, Steven. "Influence of Old Irish Beliefs on Carleton." *Carleton Newsletter* 2, no. 4 (April 4, 1972):30–31. Notes similarity between ancient ritual and Carleton's behavior.

"*Fardorougha the Miser.*" *Athenaeum,* no. 613 (July 27, 1839), p. 563. Praises the miser's characterization, greater than Balzac's Père Grandet.

Figgis, Darrell. Introduction to *Carleton's Stories of Irish Life.* Dublin: Talbot Press, 1918. Rates *Fardorougha* as his best novel.

Hooper, Charles. "A Forgotten Novelist." *Saturday Review of Literature,* April 20, 1929. Ranks Carleton with Dickens, Thackeray, and Scott. Laments that his name and work seem to be fading from public view.

Hopkins, Tighe. Introduction to *Stories by Carleton.* London: Blackie,

1905. Perceptive observation that Carleton's archetypal "mother element" allows him to accurately characterize Irish women.

Horton, Howard. "Universal Values in Irish Literature." *Carleton Newsletter* 4, no. 1 (July 4, 1973):4–5. States that Swift, Griffin, Kickham, and Carleton had an unusual understanding of human nature.

Ibarra, Eileen Sullivan (see also Eileen A. Sullivan). "The Comic Character of Fin M'Coul." *Folklore,* no. 82 (Autumn 1971), pp. 212–15. An analysis of Carleton's debunking of the heroic nature of Finn MacCumhaill, an ancient Irish hero.

———. "Folktales in Carleton's 'The Three Tasks.'" *Tennessee Folklore Society Bulletin* 36, no. 3 (September 1970):66–71. Shows association between "The Three Tasks" and elements of the universal folktale.

———. "Realistic Accounts of the Irish Peasantry in Four Novels of William Carleton." Ph.D. Dissertation; University of Florida, December 1969. Biographical data related to in-depth analysis of *Fardorougha the Miser, The Black Prophet, Valentine M'Clutchy,* and *The Emigrants of Ahadarra.*

———. "Review of Carleton's *The Black Prophet.*" *Carleton Newsletter* 4, no. 1 (July 4, 1973):6. Questions Timothy Webb's Freudian analysis of Carleton's complex nature.

———. "Thomas Davis's Criticism of Carleton's Fiction." *Carleton Newsletter* 4, no. 2 (October 4, 1973):12–14. Reprint of Davis's essays on Carleton from *Nation.*

———. "*Valentine M'Clutchy:* A Novel of Orange Terrorism in Early Nineteenth Century Northern Ireland." *Carleton Newsletter* 3, no. 3 (January 4, 1973):21–22. A review of Orange terrorist acts in the novel.

———. "William Carleton and the Picaresque Novel." *Carleton Newsletter* 1, no. 4 (April 4, 1971):27–30. Comparison between Gil Blas and Carleton, the "Irish picaro."

Jones, William. "The Evil Eye and the English Pre-Romantic Gothic Novels." *Carleton Newsletter* 1, no. 2 (October 4, 1970):12–14. Notes Gothic elements in *The Evil Eye.*

Kavanagh, Patrick. Preface to *The Autobiography of William Carleton.* London: MacGibbon & Kee, 1968. Demonstrates an awareness of Carleton's difficulties in acquiring literary fame.

Kiely, Benedict. *Modern Irish Fiction.* Dublin: Golden Eagle Books, 1950. Noteworthy critique on Carleton's works.

———. *Poor Scholar.* New York: Sheed & Ward, 1948. An excellent study of Carleton's works and life.

Leslie, Shane. Introduction to *Carleton's Country*. Dublin: Talbot Press, 1930. Comments on the vitality of characterizations in Carleton's fiction.

McHugh, Roger. "William Carleton: A Portrait of the Artist as Propagandist." *Studies* 27 (1938):47–62. Shows the ineptness of Carleton as a propagandist.

Meredith, Robert L. "William Carleton and Charles Lever." *Carleton Newsletter* 3, no. 2 (October 4, 1972):11–14. Review of Carleton's attack upon Lever's artistic integrity and characterization of Irish people.

Morrison, Richard. "A Note on William Carleton." *University Review* 31, (1964):219–26. General praise. Notes relative obscurity of Carleton's fame.

Murphy, Maureen. "Carleton and Columcille." *Carleton Newsletter* 2, no. 3 (January 4, 1972):19–21. Documents Carleton's use of the prophecyman. Notes relationship of Columcille's prophecy to beliefs held by country people in Carleton's era and in contemporary Ireland.

"National Tintings II—William Carleton." *Illustrated Dublin Journal*, no. 9 (November 2, 1861), pp. 129–32. A short account of early life, fondness for sports, reception by Catholic and Protestant clergy, and retirement to family life.

Nemo, John. "William Carleton: A Monaghan View." *Carleton Newsletter* 5, no. 2 (April 4, 1975):11–12. Reviews Patrick Kavanagh's contradictory evaluation of Carleton's fiction.

O'Brien, Edna, ed. *Some Irish Loving*. London: Weidenfeld & Nicolson, 1979. Categorizes love into various classes. *Phelim O'Toole's Courtship* falls into the intemperate class.

O'Connor, Frank. *The Backward Look, A Survey of Irish Literature*. London: Macmillan, 1967. Criticizes dialect in Carleton's fiction.

O'Donoghue, David. *The Life of William Carleton*. Vol. 2. London: Downey, 1896. A record of Carleton's life from the end of the autobiography to his death. This work is the standard source for biographical data.

O'Faolain, Sean. *The Irish: A Character Study*. New York: Devin-Adair, 1956. Discusses the priests' entrance in fiction of Carleton and others after Catholic emancipation in 1829.

Oliver, Thomas Edward. "Some Analogues of Miastre Pierre Pathelin." *Journal of American Folklore* 22 (1909):395–430. Carleton's Fin M'Coul is one analogue.

O'Sullivan, Sean. *Irish Wake Amusements.* Cork: Mercier, 1967.
Notes Carleton's description of games played at wakes.
O'Sullivan, T. F. *The Young Irelanders.* Tralee: Kerryman, 1945.
Places Carleton with Young Irelanders and discusses work written
for Library of Ireland and *Nation.*
"Recent Irish Fiction." *Citizen* 4 (October 1841):175–82. Good
critical review of *Jane Sinclair,* "The Lha Dhu or Dark Day," "The
Clarionet," and "The Dead Boxer."
Shaw, Rose. *Carleton's Country.* Dublin: Talbot Press, 1930. A
travelogue, including pictures of Clogher Valley and its
people.
Smith, G. Barnett. "A Brilliant Irish Novelist." *Fortnightly Review* 67
(1897):104–16. Praises Carleton's skill as a novelist.
Sullivan, Eileen A. (see also Eileen Sullivan Ibarra). Introduction
to *Tubber Derg, Denis O'Shaughnessy, Phelim O'Toole's Courtship,
and Neal Malone.* Florida: Renaissance Printing, 1974, 1975. Calls
attention to the Carletonian characters' sense of place and to
Carleton's humor and storytelling skill.
———. "William Carleton: Artist of Reality." *Eire-Ireland* 11, no. 4
(Winter 1976):130–40. An explanation of Carleton's perception
of reality which enabled him to capture the lifestyle of his
characters.
———. "William Carleton." *Critical Survey of Short Fiction.* Edited by
Frank Magill. Englewood Cliffs, N.J.: Salem Press, 1981, pp.
1057–63. Analysis of realistic, tragicomic, satiric, and folk-
tales.
Teague, Moyra. "Recollections of Carleton Country." *Carleton News-
letter* 3, no. 3 (January 4, 1973):20. Discusses her girlhood in
Carleton's native township. Heard little of him, a "case of neglect
of a prophet in his own country."
"Valentine M'Clutchy." *Athenaeum,* no. 898 (January 11, 1845), pp.
38–39. Believes novel was a melodramatic partisan effort for the
Repeal Association.
Warner, Alan. "Four letters from William Allingham to William
Carleton." *Carleton Newsletter* 4, no. 1 (July 4, 1979):2–3. One-
sided correspondence in which Allingham sought Carleton's
literary help and advice.
Webb, Timothy. Introduction to *The Black Prophet.* Shannon: Irish
University Press, 1972. Inaccurate analysis of Carleton's personal-
ity.
Yeats, W. B. Introduction to *Irish Fairy and Folk Tales.* New York: A.
L. Burt, n.d. Perceives Carleton's seriousness, despite the humor,
in the ghost stories.

————. Introduction to *Stories from Carleton*. London: Walter Scott, 1889. High praise for Carleton's fiction.

————. "Irish National Literature from Callahan to Carleton." *Bookman*, July 1895. Acknowledgment of Carleton's great contribution to Irish literature.

————. *The Letters of W. B. Yeats*. New York: Macmillan, 1955. Numerous references to Carleton in letters to Father Matthew Russell, Katherine Tynan, and John O'Leary. Yeats in 1899 had difficulty in locating copies of Carleton's work.

Index

Union Act of 1801, 16, 79-80,
    83, 123n1, 5

Whiteboy Society, 32-33, 92, 95
Wilde, Lady, 22
Wilde, Oscar, 22

Yeats, Jack, 83
Yeats, William B., 113
Young Irelanders, 21-22, 33,
    79, 104